SOUTH KENSINGTON MUSEUM ART HANDBOOKS.

N°. 6.—A MANUAL OF DESIGN.

MANUAL OF DESIGN

COMPILED FROM

THE WRITINGS AND ADDRESSES

OF

RICHARD REDGRAVE, R.A.,

Surveyor of Her Majesty's Pictures,

Late Inspector-General for Art, Science and Art Department,

BY

GILBERT R. REDGRAVE.

Published for the Committee of Council on Education.

SCRIBNER, WELFORD, & ARMSTRONG, NEW YORK.

CHARLES DICKENS AND EVANS,
CRYSTAL PALACE PRESS.

PREFACE.

DURING Mr. Redgrave's long and active service in connexion with the Schools of Art and the foundation of the South Kensington Museum, from which he has so lately retired, as well as in his appointed duties relating to the International Exhibitions in this country and in France, he was called upon to prepare numerous official reports. On many occasions, also, he was required, when presenting medals and prizes to the Students, to address them on the course of their studies, and on the technical training of the designer.

His reports and addresses defined and formulated many new principles of ornamental design, and contained various practical suggestions concerning the methods upon which his system of teaching had been founded. The chief of these documents which have been officially printed, are :—

1. Report on Design. Exhibition of 1851.
2. Report on Design as applied to Manufactures. Paris, 1855.
3. Report on Applications of Drawing and Modelling to the Common Arts. Paris, 1867.
4. Report on the present state of Design. Annual International Exhibition, 1871.
5. Evidence before the Commission, on the Government School of Design, 1847.
6. On the necessity of Principles in teaching Design, 1853.
7. Catalogue of Cabinet Work, Gore House, 1853.

The teaching of these reports has long been acknowledged as of recognised authority, and it has been frequently proposed that the matter contained in them should be collated and published, as it would form a useful book of reference and a manual of the principles of design.

It has been more than once suggested to me to undertake the duty; but it was not until it was formally proposed to me, by the Lords of the Committee of Council on Education, that such a work should form part of the series of South Kensington Museum Art Handbooks, that I was led with some diffidence to see how far I might be able to do justice to this task, involving, as it did, the compilation of so large a portion of the thought and labour of my father's long official career. I felt the more pleasure in attempting this work, from the gratification afforded to my father by their Lordships' selection of me, and from the assurances I received from him of his advice and assistance.

In undertaking this compilation, I have confined myself almost wholly to his own words. Indeed, nearly all the matter might be placed in inverted commas. I have studied to arrange and bring together like things in the order and upon the plan which my father has in most cases pursued, to avoid the repetitions which would naturally arise in such a series of documents, and to omit only such matters as had a local and temporary interest.

G. R. R.

May, 1876.

CONTENTS.

SECTION I.

The Principles of Ornament.

CHAPTER I.

PAGE

Preliminary Remarks 3

CHAPTER II.

On the Source of Style 12

CHAPTER III.

On the Elements of Style arising out of Construction . 29

CHAPTER IV.

On Utility, which must be considered before Decoration . 36

CHAPTER V.

On Fitness of the Ornament to the Material to which it is applied 43

CHAPTER VI.

On Unity of Style and Decorative subordination . . . 48

SECTION II.

The Application of the Principles of Ornament to the Manufactures.

CHAPTER VII.

PAGE

ON THE NATURE AND GENERAL APPLICATION OF ORNAMENTAL ART 55

CHAPTER VIII.

ON THE DECORATION OF BUILDINGS 65

CHAPTER IX.

ON DOMESTIC AND OTHER FURNITURE 87

CHAPTER X.

ON DOMESTIC UTENSILS AND OBJECTS OF PERSONAL USE . . 112

CHAPTER XI.

ON THE DECORATION OF GARMENT FABRICS 133

SECTION III.

The Teaching of Ornament, and the Education of the Designer.

CHAPTER XII.

ON ART EDUCATION IN THIS COUNTRY AND ABROAD 155

CHAPTER XIII.

ON THE SPECIAL EDUCATION OF THE DESIGNER 169

SECTION I.

THE PRINCIPLES OF ORNAMENT.

A MANUAL OF DESIGN.

CHAPTER I.

PRELIMINARY REMARKS.

THERE are certain periods in the history of the world or of individual nations, when some important event, some discovery, or some cause which deeply affects the public mind, produces a corresponding change in art also. Such for instance, in civilised Europe, was the change produced by the discovery of printing and the dissemination by its means of the writings and thoughts of the ancients. These led to the study and contemplation of those fragments of antique art which had survived the injuries of time and barbarism, and the result of their study was to reconstitute beauty as the prevailing principle of art: they led also to the subversion of the religious sentiment which had, for many ages, been the leading and all-pervading idea of art.

Again, when from political changes art became gradually estranged from its Italian cradle, to be fostered by the growing power of the French kings; and when the victories of the Fourteenth Louis had gained him the title of the Great Monarch, art also was led captive in his triumph. No longer satisfied with beauty, she decked herself to please him in "barbaric pomp and gold": splendour and display became her ruling principles, and the Louis Quatorze style called after his name was formed.

As we approach still nearer to our own æra other changes, not so marked, but equally characteristic, might be noticed as influencing art through changes in the outer and surrounding world: all these changes are clearly discernible to us who look back upon them; we can even trace them to apparent causes; but rising gradually and imperceptibly in their own age, they were then not clearly noted as points of departure, as they did not sufficiently influence the prevailing taste to form a new and distinctive style.

In any critical examination of the present state of design, our attention is in the first place forcibly directed towards France, which has long ruled our taste in such matters. It may, therefore, be as well in the first place to glance at the conditions which have led to this state of things, and caused our neighbours for so long a period to rule supreme in matters of taste.

The decorative arts, attracted to France by Francis the First, were actively patronized and encouraged by the succeeding House of Bourbon. Colbert, the Minister of the great Louis, established, as royal manufactories, the tapestry and furniture works of the Gobelins, Beauvais, and Aubusson, and in these works the most skilled workmen, aided by the most scientific men of the age, executed the designs of the first artists of France. In the succeeding reign the porcelain works of Sèvres became also a royal establishment with the like appliances for artistic excellence.

In these royal manufactories every effort was made to attain the highest degree of perfection, and the works were carried on with princely munificence, entirely irrespective of the cost of production. By Colbert also, schools for the instruction of the workmen in drawing and the elements of art were organized in some of the principal seats of French manufactures.

By these means France, and more especially Paris, gradually became looked up to for works of luxury. The products of her royal manufactories were spread abroad among the other nations of Europe, either by purchase, or as gifts to the various monarchs and princes, and the skilled labours of French workmen gradually led the surrounding countries to recognize her as the school of the decorative arts, and the acknowledged arbitress of taste.

The Revolution, and the long wars that succeeded it, though repressing for a time the intercourse with France, did not deprive her of those institutions which had tended thus to advance her in the eyes of the nations, neither did they disperse the continuous band of skilled workmen and cunning artificers who would emanate from these factories to raise still higher the pretensions of France to be considered the chief source of objects of luxury and taste.

To the protracted wars which had divided this Island from the Continent, and in many respects the Continental nations from each other, succeeded an equally long peace, during which commerce increased, and the accumulating wealth of Europe became everywhere invested in those vast undertakings which facilitate the intercourse of nations. By these means we were led insensibly to the first of those gatherings which were to bring together in one place all that science, skilled labour, and the arts could produce, and by which each country endeavours to supply the growing wants, and to tempt the increasing taste for luxury in its own and other lands.

It was under this natural tendency of the age, and arising out of it, that the first great gathering of the national industries took place in 1851. It took place, not inappropriately, in our own country, which had most diligently laboured in the improvement of the means of intercourse, and had most actively promoted the free communication of nations, by the construction of railroads and ships, and the removal of commercial restrictions.

To this first Exhibition, France, our nearest neighbour, was, after ourselves, the greatest contributor, and especially so in those objects for which she had so long held a high reputation. The first gathering of the industries of the world was speedily followed by a second in France itself.

In this second Exhibition the fine arts were more fully associated with industry as an integral portion of the Exhibition than in 1851, and the artists of Europe who had been invited—painters, sculptors, and architects—largely responded to the call. The entire of the arts thus formed a most judicious addition, and one which gave a marked character to the First Paris Universal Exhibition, inasmuch as the reciprocal influence of the arts on manufacture could be carefully examined.

Former periods of advance in the products of the artizan in any country have always been connected with progress in the fine arts, and there is reason to believe that taste and skill in manufactures are seldom attained by a country in which the fine arts are neglected, or not properly cultivated or encouraged. Here then was afforded an opportunity on a grand scale to consider the two in their mutual relations, and to examine the assembled products of the manufacturer and the artizan, together with those of the artists of the several countries; in order to test if the inspirations of the latter had indeed led the others to a higher degree of taste, excellence, and skilful manipulation.

It has been already noticed that great public events, and the changed characteristics of the age, result in marked epochs of art and industry; and it is not too much to believe that these great international exhibitions, arising out of and consequent upon the scientific improvements of the age and upon the improved means of intercourse, may conduce to some such important change in public taste. In these exhibitions the manufacturers of all countries are striving to compete, not so much in works of ordinary excellence, as in the production of such as shall outvie each other, and be considered markedly in advance of the taste and skill of the times. The result of these competitive struggles must be an advance to real excellence, or a retrograde movement towards decline, according as they are made on sound, or on ill-understood principles.

There would, however, be little difficulty in showing that, in former periods, the introduction of one false principle in decorative art, diverging at first but slightly from the truth, has led gradually to the entire adoption of a false, vitiated, and meretricious style. It is therefore most necessary that nothing should be taken upon trust, but that a searching investigation should be made at the present time, lest we are led astray by the grandeur of these displays, the vast amount of skilled labour, and the gorgeousness of the materials used, to accept the false for the true, the meretricious for the excellent, or the gaudy for the magnificent. We must not allow the blandishments of false and meretricious excellence, or of skill misapplied, to hinder the condemnation of works, however rare the talent displayed on them, but rather the reverse, for mediocrity will rarely lead us astray; it is the sins of genius that lead the multitude to do evil, and in such cases the more the talent the greater the crime.

On entering upon such an examination it must be remembered that there are many difficulties in the way of a just judgment. As has been remarked, such exhibitions, however much it may be desired that they should do so, hardly represent the normal state of the manufacture. Each manufacturer is striving his utmost to attain notice and reward, not so much, it is to be feared, by an effort after perfect taste in his goods, as by an endeavour to catch the consumers by startling novelty or meretricious decoration, leading, in most cases, to an extreme redundancy of ornament. The goods are like the gilded cakes in the booths of our country fairs, no longer for use, but to attract customers.

Moreover, in endeavouring to form a just estimate of European manufactures the differences of national taste must not be overlooked. It will be universally allowed that the French as a people are more deeply imbued with the love of and the desire for ornament than other nations of Europe, and that, as compared with this country, the general knowledge of the middle and lower classes of Paris is, in such matters, above that of the same rank in England.

For this there are many causes, arising from political circumstances, climate, mode of living, and a hundred other things wherein they differ from us islanders.

Family life abroad differs so entirely from what it is in England. In the case of our nearest neighbours the French, what we understand by home-life is almost unknown—lofty erections of several stories permit several families to live under one roof, and without great cost to the tenant a more decorative treatment of the general structure is rendered possible. The places of general entertainment, intended for the pleasure of the many, are richly decorated, and each individual lives more or less in public, and in the enjoyment of public splendours.

The taste of successive monarchs, suiting itself to the genius of the people, has led to the erection of magnificent palaces in Paris and its environs, and the talent of the greatest artists of France has from time to time been engaged to decorate them. Rich in carvings, in costly marbles, in gilding and painting, in mirrors and arabesques, these palaces contain also collections of the rarest pictures and the finest sculptures of the artists of all ages. They are at certain times open to the people, and on fêtes and holidays are crowded, as a matter of right, by all classes, from the *ouvrier* in his blouse to the shopkeeper, the merchant, and the man of fashion.

These great national works, the constant sight of which has stimulated the public taste for ornament and decorative enrichment, have been the school for a body of skilled artists and workmen capable of gratifying the taste thus fostered, and we find that many of the theatres, the cafés, the restaurants, and even the shops of Paris, in the richness of their decoration and the splendour of their gilding, vie with the palaces, which they attempt to rival.

But all this decoration constantly around the Parisian, imbuing him unconsciously with a knowledge of and taste for ornament, and insensibly forming his inclinations and educating his eye, has its defects as well as its advantages.

Accustomed to gaze on the splendour, the gorgeous enrichments of palaces, to sit weekly in their salons on velvet couches, not alone to enjoy the chastened art of the great works that adorn their walls, but to feast his eyes on the gilded blandishments of the chambers in which these works of art are enshrined; accustomed also to the glittering brilliancy of his café, adorned for his delectation, and in many senses of the word more his home than the nightly dormitory he retires to from them, he cannot be content in his own house with the simple furniture suitable to his rank. His small apartments are fitted up for show rather than for *comfort*, a word not in his language : everything must simulate his out-of-door experiences, and if he cannot afford realities he will obtain the appearance of them by gaudy finery and over-decoration. In his commodes, his armoires, his hangings, his couches, his pendules, and his candelabra, utility is too often overlooked in favour of display and ornamentation.

Taste, therefore, which is in accordance with the habits, inclinations, and general disposition of any people, may be *national* without being *correct*. It is with nations as it is with individuals concerning whom we hear it said that one has a vulgar taste, another a refined taste, one a mean taste, another a taste for the beautiful or the magnificent. Thus in referring to the ancients, all who have had any knowledge of ancient art or literature would at once say that the Greeks as a people had a taste for the refined and the beautiful; in literature, always entering into the most subtile definitions and the nicest distinctions, and in art, refining all they undertook with the most sensitive perception of what is perfect; never leaving a new creation until they had by continual effort arrived at the most beautiful form, proportion, and colour of which it was capable.

The Romans, who succeeded to their art, were of a different temperament: grandeur and massiveness were the leading characteristics of their taste. Larger in mind than the Greeks, there was at the same time a coarse strength in their nature; and a barbaric grandeur to which Greek art never attained, was the corresponding result. This was shown in the vast extent of their public buildings (such as the Baths of Titus and the Coliseum, compared with which the largest works of the Greeks would appear diminutive), in the coarse vigour and bold relief of their ornamentation, and the spherical curves of their mouldings.

Thus we see, that while each nation had a taste, the taste of each was wholly different; and in examining French taste, which has so long dominated over the nations of Europe, it is most desirable thoroughly to search into its principles, that we may know when it is worthy of being admitted and followed, and when it is to be rejected, in order that a higher, purer, and more simple taste may be sought after in its stead.

We have already shown that French art is accommodated to the mind of the French people, and reacts upon it; that it is up to their requirements, mental and sentimental, and certainly not beyond them. Whatever it might have formerly done, it now ministers to the inclinations of the people, but does not lead them. The French are a pleasure-loving people, of a gay and lively disposition, with a sensuous indulgence in pleasurable enjoyments, a proper national vanity and a love of display. To this their whole industrial art ministers; and from all causes, natural and induced, the tendency of the national taste is evidently to glitter and over-ornamentation to display and finery rather than to decorated usefulness. We repeat therefore that it is most desirable as France has been so long acknowledged as the arbitress of European taste and fashion that we should test thoroughly the ground of her pretensions, and should beware lest unconsciously "the world is still deceived with ornament," and led astray by pretentious display, instead of advancing in the road to real excellence.

The first step in this direction will be to attempt to lay down some general principles of taste in decoration, deduced from those works which in all ages have been considered excellent. Without such principles for our guidance, the inquiry would descend into vague and unsatisfactory assertions, a course which has fostered the idea that taste has no settled laws, but is a mere matter of fashion or individual feeling, against which there is neither dispute nor appeal.

CHAPTER II.

ON THE SOURCE OF STYLE.

In attempting to define the principles which should govern decorative design, the first consideration must be given to those dominating influences, which pervading all the works of a period, subordinate them to what is called STYLE. These influences, as we have already seen, may, and indeed must be various: they generally arise out of circumstances which impress the universal mind of the age, or of some nation pre-eminently great in learning, rule, manufacture, commerce, or the arts.

Style, indeed, will be universal in proportion as the sentiment which inspires it is more or less widely prevalent, more or less akin to our common nature; and on this account those styles which have arisen out of the religious sentiment are generally co-extensive with the religion which produced them.

When these influences arise out of the purer and nobler qualities of man's nature, the style they produce will be noble also, and being constantly around us, contribute in no small degree to raise the tone of individual and national feeling. The influence of a mean style, founded upon the ignoble or sensual qualities, will in a like degree tend to degrade not only our taste but our moral intellect also.

Thus the governing influences of Greece, when her art was formed, were the worship of the Deity through his created forms and attributes of *beauty*; and a sentiment of purity and beauty became the characteristics of Greek art. In the latter days of this people, when the poetical religion gave way before the subtilty of her philosophers, the sense of the beautiful only remained, and the principle of her art, deprived of the zealous fire that even an imperfect religious sentiment inspires, became more sensual under the domination of abstract beauty only.

When the Greeks were conquered by the Romans, and their artists transplanted to serve the conquerors, they brought with them their own dominant principle, sensuous beauty. This, however, alone, ill suited the spirit of their proud rulers. In the full career of universal conquest, pomp and splendour were their governing influences, and a new style was formed, wherein a degree of barbarous grandeur dominated over the element of beauty.

As the Romans, from being the conquerors, in turn became the conquered, their art died out under the mean and contemptible desire to appear what they no longer were; having no influence sufficiently strong to inspire their artists, they became degraded imitators, and even broke down the mighty works of their fathers, to build trophies to call after their own names. The all-pervading spirit which had been present in the growth of Roman art being gone, Europe was ready for the new influence, which, gradually working on society, was to pervade all the nations in various degrees with the spirit of Christianity, and to produce the new styles called Romanesque and Gothic, wherein the sentiment of religion again largely prevailed.

And perhaps the very circumstance that religion was presented by means of art materially to the senses, rather than spiritually to the reason and intellect, increased the universality of the influence. Not only had the churches, but even the houses and all the worldly goods of our fathers, the outward impress of these new styles, which appearing first in the erection and decoration of splendid temples devoted to the worship of the Deity, gradually gave to all things an ecclesiastical character also.

When, from the causes before glanced at, the renaissance of ancient art took place, it was impossible that any sentiment of religion, which, in its own age, it might have possessed, could be re-born with it; the beautiful only was sought in this revival;—beauty, however, more or less tainted with the sensuality and pride of the peoples from the study of whose remains the resurrection to new life had been attempted.

Revived moreover without a thorough identity between the sentiment of the age, and the sentiment of the past which produced it, this style became at once subject to national modifications. In our own country it resulted in the Tudor, a style redundant yet mean and grotesque; without ingenuity, and without any constructive truth or consistency. It bore the impress of a people willing to borrow their art at second-hand rather than endeavour to cultivate it at home. Flemish, Italian, and French versions of the renaissance were mixed up in a strange medley with the Gothic of the preceding age, and the style had a character arising out of its very errors and absurdities.

In France the renaissance was gradually modified by successive monarchs, until the revived love of beauty which had given it re-birth gave place to the sentiment of pride. It was modified to pander to the self-esteem of the monarchs and people of the age, and mere meretricious splendour resulted in that style which is called the style of Louis Quinze. In all that this style differed from the true renaissance, it differed merely as arising out of decoration, and from the love for mere magnificence and display, for which it was admirably adapted, being one of the most suitable styles for gilding, and for brilliancy and sparkle in metal and or-molu work; showy and glittering beyond anything attainable in the simpler forms of the renaissance or of classic antiquity.

It must however be allowed to have a sufficiency of marked characteristics to rank as an acknowledged style; the last in order which decorative art has developed, and, with the other instances brought together, tends to establish that one of the first elements of true style is an all-pervading and over-ruling sentiment.

In considering the elements of *style*, it must be remembered, that style does not merely relate to decoration, as is too often supposed, but originates in construction, to which decoration is only subsidiary. All the great æras of style have been notedly æras of changed construction. The mound-like temples of Egypt, the horizontal constructions of Greece, the arched vaultings of Rome, the vertical aspirings of Gothic buildings, contain elements of STYLE as marked in their *bare walls*, as when, in their completed state, they are covered with the rich decorative treatments peculiar to them.

These preliminary arguments being admitted, it will follow, first, that style implies some dominating influence reflecting the mind of the age in all its works, and therefore presumes a certain unity of character throughout.

Secondly, that the primary elements of style are constructive, and that the design of a work must have regard to construction, and consequently to proper use of materials, prior to the consideration of its ornamental decoration.

Thirdly, that as construction necessarily implies a purpose, *utility* must have the precedence of decoration.

Fourthly, as construction necessitates a proper consideration of materials, and as each material has its own mode of manipulation, and is wrought by separate and varied processes; design must be bad which applies indiscriminately the same constructive forms or ornamental treatments to materials differing in their nature and application.

Fifthly, that as the greater regulates the lesser, the building should determine the style, and all which it contains of furniture or decoration should conform to its characteristics; and thus there would be a proper uniformity of style throughout, and a subordination of all the inferior objects to one another and to the whole.

Many minor principles are contained under each of these several propositions. In the few words of discussion on each necessary to connect them with our present subject, these will be noticed, and it is hoped that the preliminary argument will lead to a better understanding of the whole question of decorative design as illustrated subsequently in our remarks upon our various manufactures.

The subject of the first proposition—the prevailing influence characterizing works and thus producing style, has already been touched upon. When this influence is neither strong nor general, characteristic indications of style will be slight and hardly noticeable, and the age will be imitative rather than original : even the slight national character that is present in art labours being less observable by the people themselves than by others.

Thus although to Englishmen there appeared so little originality in the art applied to our own manufactures at Paris in the International Exhibition of 1855 as to incline us to regard them as devoid of any peculiar character, we were less at a loss to perceive a nationality in those produced in Germany, France, or Spain. It was some satisfaction, therefore, on various occasions to hear the same remark from Frenchmen and others on the manufactures of their own land, namely, that they could recognize national characteristics, and many indications of novelty and unity of style in British goods, these qualities being absent to them in their own ; a subject which seemed most justly a cause of regret on their part. Our mutual remarks are therefore somewhat encouraging to each other, and we may hope that there are influences at work to raise us above the rank of mere imitators of the men of other lands and other times—and as imitators necessarily shortcomers—and that we may thus impress the national character of our age and people on our art and our works.

The great effort that is now made towards a wide-spread development of art education in Great Britain—and this not alone for the upper and middle classes, but for all, even the poorest, must tell upon the rising generation. Once properly instructed, there is very little doubt that the plain good sense, the energy of will, and the dislike of mere display of our countrymen will result in works of much higher excellence in decorative art than has yet been attained in this country. The artizan will thus be empowered to add to his admitted manual dexterity and thorough workmanship, the knowledge and taste that will enable him to join beauty to excellence, and to carry out the labours which the advanced taste of the general public will demand at his hands.

It has been said above that we are rarely sensible of our own growth and progress, and thus it is most difficult to estimate whether any sentiment arising amongst us is sufficiently strong, persistent, and all-prevailing to produce a style. Such, however, may be the case notwithstanding our lack of the power to perceive it. There seem to be many symptoms that the desired change is arising, and will arise out of, or be very materially influenced by the great scientific improvements and discoveries of our times. Not however directly, but indirectly. Changed materials are altering the whole system of construction, and utility, in such works, is of necessity a paramount consideration; the iron road has opened up to the multitude the power of seeing and enjoying nature; the camera fixes her most fleeting images, and allows us to surround ourselves with evidences of the marvellous and infinite variety of her beauties; the art of nature-printing places the very accidents of growth and structure palpably before us. As the altered character of the materials, and the necessity of strictly considering utility in our scientific works, has improved our knowledge of structure and weaned us from mere precedents in constructive art; so the opportunity of seeing and enjoying nature, and of searching into the details of her beautiful variety, has led to such a love and delight in natural objects as may be productive of a new style in decorative art also. If these sources of novelty are rightly understood and directed, they point indeed to a most hopeful future, if due regard is paid to the principles of ornamental adaptation hereafter to be laid down.

If there was any perceptible advance towards novelty in design in the great Exhibition of 1851, it was the tendency to *naturalistic* treatments of ornament, pervading not only those fabrics wherein imitative renderings are easily adapted, but those manufactures also in which the primary consideration of structure and use required at least some modification in the application of Nature's details to manufactures—as, for instance, in furniture and metal-work. As an indication, however, of an increased love of nature, and of recurrence to her, as the true source of ornamental decoration, this tendency, notwithstanding its errors, may be hailed with satisfaction; and our endeavours should be earnestly directed to avoid former faults, and to teach the *right* mode of seeing and making use of nature. This must be accomplished not by the mere imitative rendering of flowers and foliage, which is a means of study, but not the end: the ornamentist must be a much deeper student, if he would found a new style. If he seeks out the mode of development of vegetable growth, he will find that regularity and symmetry are the normal laws, while all that is irregular is accidental and extraneous.

This is in strict accordance with the principles of ornament in the best times; indeed, in this lies the true distinction between pictorial and ornamental art; that which has been called disparagingly *naturalistic* ornament, arises from the ornamentist forgetting his own laws, and the absolute laws of natural growth, and taking to mere pictorial imitation, which regards the accidents and disturbances of growth only.

These normal laws would instruct the ornamentist that nature is developed in strict geometrical and numerical rhythm. Thus leaves are placed on the supporting stem either continuously opposite, or alternate, or numerically recurrent; and as are the leaves, so are the future stems placed also. Again, varied quantity would be learnt from the study of nature; while it would be found that all vegetation is developed under a law of numbers; those numbers most largely prevail whose correspondent geometric forms give the greatest variety consistent with symmetry. Thus three, corresponding with the triangle, is the law of inflorescence of all endogenous vegetation, whilst the flowers of exogens are developed numerically as five, corresponding with the pentagon, much more largely than as four, the less varied root of the square; thus contributing to the greatest amount of symmetry consistent with variety.

Moreover, the ornamentist might learn something of restraint, and be warned against over-ornamentation, by seeing how nature restricts her true ornaments, the flowers, to the most salient and culminating points of plants, and sprinkles them sparingly, contrasted with the foliage. It is not in place here to allude to the colours of nature, because the endeavour is simply to prove that the principle of symmetrical arrangement, advocated as the true law of ornament, is to be deduced from the study of nature's laws of growth. Our aim, while referring to the hope that an increased acquaintance with nature may be operating to produce a style, is to insist upon the necessity of a thorough examination of and not a mere superficial acquaintance with her works: we shall then find "the art itself is nature," and that as Shakespeare tells us—

> "Nature is made better by no mean,
> But nature makes that mean; so o'er that art,
> Which you say adds to nature, is an art
> That nature makes."

There was ever a true sense of ornamental distribution in the early Italian works which extended even to pictorial art when applied decoratively to walls, the principle being derived from Byzantine sources. This principle was not wholly neglected by artists so late as the time of Francia and Bartoloméo, as is evidenced in their balanced and symmetrical compositions. When, however, pictorial art began to assert itself over the decorative, and to assume its own high place and office, then the ornamental principle succumbed to pictorial treatment, and the painted ornament, as well as much also of the ornamental sculpture of the early renaissance, became pictorial and unsymmetrical. This will at once be seen by anyone who examines the bas-reliefs, or even the fruit and foliage of the architrave of the Florentine gates by Ghiberti. Herein pictorial art reigns paramount; the frieze which surrounds the gates is an imitative rendering of nature, hardly disposed according to the law of

FIG. I.

geometrical distribution; even the bas-reliefs are pictorial not sculpturesque: many planes enter into their composition; so that it may be said that the painter rather than the sculptor—the artist certainly rather than the ornamentist—has composed them. The return to classic examples stayed the innovation for a time in sculpture of the cinquecento period; but the irregular treatment became more dominant than ever in the 17th century.

It must be admitted that there are styles dependent for their character on the absence both of symmetry and of constructive truth. The style called after Louis Quatorze ignores all constructive truth :—Supporting forms are twisted and have even their continuity broken, and in the ornamental details symmetry is purposely disregarded, the aim evidently being to startle or surprise us by novelty and magnificence. Thus rich veneers, costly marbles, finely chased or-molu, with a profusion of gilding, give a meretricious splendour viciously alluring and dangerous to young designers. We reproduce here a sofa (Fig. 1), from Assilineau, to illustrate the foregoing observations.

FIG. 2.

The opening of Japan also has brought the art of this people more prominently before us of late; an art which rejects symmetry as a principle. But in the beautiful productions of this art-sensitive people, the absence of symmetry is compensated for by their refined feeling for balance of quantity, both of form and of colour—and this, aided by its novelty and from its very quaintness, makes us overlook the distortion arising from the unsymmetrical construction of their furniture. Eventually, however, even here the absence of symmetry is felt to be an error in principle. The little cabinet (Fig. 2) will serve as an illustration of the Japanese irregular treatment.

Yet from what has been said, it must be evident that the law of symmetrical arrangement is not only in accordance with a deeper insight into nature's working, but moreover lends itself to the absolute necessities of many manufactures, especially in this age of machinery, and proves the best means for the display of form and colour in all. The naturalistic view on the other hand is not only difficult of execution in many manufactures and fabrics, but is a mere surface view of nature, only concerning itself with what is open to every one, and neglecting those hidden truths which lie at the root of the whole subject.

That man's love of nature who studies her inmost secrets to apply them anew to his handiwork, must be much more intense than his who only looks at her to make false and exaggerated imitations of roses, poppies, and peonies, to sprawl them over carpets and who reverses even her simplest laws to stand brass candlesticks on the points of leaves; who causes gas to jet out of the corollas of flowers, or who covers with bunches of grapes or sprays of ivy the fronts of cabinets or buffets. The one studies nature, the other caricatures her.

It is in this spirit of a loving study of nature, coupled with a due appreciation for art, that the courses in our public art schools are now arranged. Alternately with the study of ornament, the pupil has natural foliage, fruit, and flowers placed before him; he is taught to imitate natural objects carefully, then to investigate the laws of their growth and development; and finally, as a step to invention, he is instructed how to arrange according to like geometrical laws and principles the unnumbered beautiful forms and varied colours with which nature supplies him.

Moreover, many able writers and earnest workmen in this country have of late years endeavoured to inculcate the true principles of decorative art, and of the application of nature's forms to ornament; and a general sense of the truth of these principles begins to prevail.

The question of the direct imitation, or the conventional treatment of natural objects as the details of ornament, has been of late much discussed, and requires indeed the fullest consideration, if, as has been suggested, there is a likelihood that the electrotype and the camera are leading, through a deeper insight into nature, to novelty of style; while a recurrence to nature for new elements is enforced in our schools.

It must be remembered that absolute imitation, difficult in fine art, is almost impossible in many manufactures, whether produced by hand or by the machine, and therefore imitation can be but a question of degree. Take for instance the application of art more peculiarly to manufacture by machinery; say in the case of calico-printing. Here the precise imitation of natural objects is impossible, since relief is unattainable, although the appearance of relief may be given by light, shade, perspective, and colour. But is the mode or degree of imitation peculiar to the artist flower-painter that which is most suitable or conducive to the desired end? In the first place, the processes of production control the application of colour, which must be laid on in separate and unblended masses by means of machinery, and not by that curious and delicate instrument the human hand, while the several tints also must be applied by successive and distinct processes; so that it would seem scarcely possible that calico-printing could compete with the imitative means at the disposal of the flower-painter.

Let us, however, allow that by improved mechanical and scientific aids the imitation of flowers, foliage, or other natural objects in light, shadow, growth, colour, and relief could be rendered as perfect by machinery as it is by a Van Huysum or a Daniel Seghers; still the art is to be applied to a specific use, and not to be examined as a picture is. The fabric on which the painting is to be impressed is partly transparent, and the forms are at once blurred and indistinct; the garment it is intended to be made into is to hang full and in folds; thus the light, shade, and the very forms of the object which has been imitated, are confused and hidden, and that *imitation* which the manufacturer has been at such pains to produce is entirely lost and destroyed. The garment moves with every motion of the wearer, and any examination of this rare art, as we are enabled to examine the painter's work, is, by the very use of the material, as impossible as it is undesirable.

Printing again necessitates a constant repetition of the same details; and what would be said of the painter who, instead of a rare flower or group of flowers, offered for our admiration a dozen or a hundred, of the same monotonous form, the same unvaried colour, the same tedious arrangement of imitation? if the painter's imitation is sought for by the calico-printer;—let at least each flower, each sprig, each group, be varied and different. But, no; such is not the end in view: it is not to imitate the painter, it is not to attempt to vie with nature that is the true aim of the calico-printer. The legitimate art to be applied to such fabrics is at once seen to be simply to decorate or enrich the surface with agreeable forms and colours, and if for this purpose we employ the beautiful forms and colours of natural objects, it must be consistently with the true use and purpose of the material and with the means at our command to produce the effect sought for. As the machinery by which the art is reproduced acts by a constant repetition, a geometrical distribution of forms is more or less a necessity which cannot be overcome. As the tints must be laid on separately and successively, and cannot be softened or blended, the simplest combination of tints and colours must be sought for rather than the more intricate; a condition necessitated also in point of cost and called for by the market offered for such goods.

If varied hues of colour are introduced; to be agreeable to

the eye, colour must be distributed according to fixed laws of quantity and juxta-position; and this is scarcely attainable by that mode of imitation which is called naturalistic, while it lends itself readily to that symmetrical and regular display of the plant which is called a "conventional treatment," a treatment shown to be consistent with the natural laws of the growth of plants, as it is also with that simple impression which flowers in their natural state of growth make on the casual observer.

It has been already said that direct imitation of nature pertains to fine art, but not to ornament other than as a means of study. Even in fine art, imitation, although the necessary language of the art, is impertinent and mean when it becomes the end sought, or as an eloquent writer has expressed it, "so degrading a thing is deception even in the approach or appearance of it, that all painting which even reaches the mark of apparent realization is degraded in so doing." (Ruskin, Seven Lamps, p. 31.) Thus we acknowledge at once the sublimity and grandeur of Rembrandt, the deep mysteries of his generalised imitation of nature's great truths, while we despise the mean littleness of his pupil Dow, who wasted the capabilities of his art in the deceptive treatment of the rind of an onion, the knitting of a stocking, or in producing hair by hair the texture of fur.

The sculptor, moreover, does not seek deceptive imitation, but rather the normal form only; otherwise it would not be necessary to consider if the colouring of flesh or draperies was permissible to the statuary: it would, as being the nearest approach to deceptive imitation, be the highest effort of his art. Such, however, is not the case; and although the ignorant are in the habit of making imitative deception a ground of wonder, the more intelligent and educated have consented to place it very low in the scale of artistic qualifications, and to agree with the assertion "that no art is noble which in any way depends on direct imitation for its effect on the mind."

But if mere imitation is inconsistent with nobility in fine art, it is also as inconsistent with the principles as it is with the means at command in ornamental art, which seeks either symbolic expression, or the merely beautiful, or both in combination. Its forms and colours of beauty and richness must be derived from nature, but are not of necessity copies of her works. "Symbolic expression," as has been said, "appeals altogether to thoughts, and in noways trusts to realization." Thus the well-known wave scroll of the Greeks was not imitative: it truly symbolized the ever-recurring waves of their inland sea, but at the same time it was an abstract form of beauty also. This was indeed the case with all their ornament; they chose, no doubt, the most elegant forms from leaf and flower, but they cared not to preserve the least actual resemblance to the type they copied. Their ornament was all abstractedly beautiful, the most elegant and refined curves being chosen and the most rigid symmetry observed; sometimes as simply recurrent as in the wave scroll; sometimes alternately recurrent, as in the anthemion and tulip form of the frieze of the Erectheum, but always rhythmical.

The Egyptians, although deriving the details of their ornament more evidently from nature, still treated them strictly as ornament and arranged them accordingly; and not to tire with instances, the Jews (to whom, if there ever was a true inspiration of genius, we are to believe such inspiration was given), deriving their ornament from natural objects, were taught by divine command to arrange it symmetrically and in a continuous order, the robe of their Ephod being bordered with "a golden bell and a pomegranate, a golden bell and a pomegranate upon the hem of the robe round about."

These principles of symmetry—of conventional treatment—and geometrical arrangement were handed down to us from the nations of antiquity through the Byzantine ornamentists, and prevailed almost exclusively in Romanesque decoration, and largely, if less decidedly so, in Gothic. If such laws of arrangement were necessary when ornament was produced by handicraft labour, how much more so are they in our age of production by machinery. In all ornament so produced, whether by printing, stamping, or weaving, some law of geometrical recurrence, both of form and colour, is enforced by the requisite *repeats*, and takes place, however we may strive to disguise it, at oft-recurring intervals; and the question is whether we shall strive to ignore and hide it in efforts after *pictorial art*, or whether it is not more judicious to accept it as a law and make it subservient to our own purposes, in the extended use now more than ever advocated, of nature's treasures.

While on the subject of style we must remember that old styles are, and perhaps ever will be imitated: and indeed the larger number of modern works are based upon imitations; but the mere imitation of past works will not renew or give real vitality to an old style. In order to do this, the artist must enter into the spirit of the past age, and be imbued with the same feelings that then prevailed; and not only the artist, but the world also for whom he labours. The artist must go with the spirit of his own time, or be strong enough to lead it, and this can only be done by an earnest and convinced will. Indeed, it must be allowed that in general the age as much makes the artist as the artist the age. Even in reproductions of old styles, national character has much to do with the result; thus in English works some sympathy with the Gothic is largely evident, while in France the styles reproduced are mostly the cinquecento renaissance, and that of Louis XIV. and XV.

It appears a curious anomaly, although, as has been shown it is really very consistent with the French character, that in France, a Catholic country, there is so little tendency to revert to the truly ecclesiastical styles. The direction of French taste is certainly not to the Gothic, far less so indeed than is the case in Protestant England. Even in those objects and utensils which are for the service of the Church, the Gothic style is rarely used, the Romanesque occurs perhaps more frequently, while there is a strong tendency to take renaissance types for these purposes, not only in chalices, flagons, monstrances, &c., but also in altar work. And yet the renaissance is essentially a sensuous style, and far more fitted for the banqueting-table than for the altar.

CHAPTER III.

ON THE ELEMENTS OF STYLE ARISING OUT OF CONSTRUCTION.

THE second preposition states that the primary elements of *style* are constructive, and that the design of a work must have regard to construction, and consequently to the proper use of materials, prior to the consideration of its ornamental decoration. That the primary elements of style are constructive will at once be manifest when it is remembered that the constructive application of materials gives the broad distinction between the architecture of the ancient and of the modern world.

The ancient races sought grandeur and sublimity by building temples formed of enormous masses of stone simply imposed on one another, the remains of which we still gaze at with wonder and surprise. It is true that the feeling inspired is of the earth, earthy, the building of necessity clings to earth: we think less of the gods that were honoured by these labours than of the men that wrought them; yet, looking upon the huge cyclopean walls, the monolithic pillars, and the enormous lintels of these mighty structures, we acknowledge that, if man is magnified rather than God, "there were giants on the earth in those days." Such is the horizontal system of construction.

Our Gothic fathers wrought altogether in another spirit; in all their doings they were looking upwards. Like the Israelites of old, each had his own offering, each as it were brought his gift to the altar, his stone to the building, and lifted it higher and higher towards the God of heaven, to whom the sacrifice was made, and who alone was to be magnified by the work. Such is the vertical system of construction, differing alike in the sentiment that inspired it and in the mode of using the materials of construction, and consequently in all the elements of style.

The primary consideration of construction is so necessary to pure design, that it may be taken as a rule that whenever style and ornament are found to be debased, it will be seen that constructive truth was first disregarded, and that those styles which are considered the purest; and the best periods of those styles, are just those wherein constructive utility has been rightly understood, and most fully attended to. Thus in the masterpieces of Gothic architecture, the necessities of construction produced much of the decoration; for instance, flying and other buttresses and pinnacles, constructively necessary to resist the thrusts of the inner groined work and roof, were by the skill of the Gothic architect rendered strikingly beautiful and ornamental features, materially ministering to character. In castellated architecture also, the battlements and machicolations, at first constructed for use, were made to contribute largely to enrichment.

On the contrary, the renaissance architect being in too many cases but the mere revivalist of ancient classic constructive details, was obliged in order to apply these details to modern uses to resort to continual constructive shams and falsities.

The introduction of the arch into construction by the Romans had tended, even in their own age, to modify the ancient principle, and when classic architecture was revived at the æra of the renaissance, the men of those days, who had seen the Gothic temple in its glory, were tempted to endeavour still more to unite the horizontal with the perpendicular principle. The two thoughts, however, are essentially distinct, as are all the constructive details they lead to, and a mixed or composite system of architecture is not to be formed by taking the ranges of columns, the porticoes, and roof-formed pediments of classic architecture, and piling them one upon another, as a child raises higher and higher his house of cards. If such a mixed style is to be arrived at, it can only be accomplished by an entirely new departure, by some master-mind starting from the constructive root, thence building up the necessary parts, and gradually decorating the construction as it arises.

Half the gross faults of bad styles may fairly be traced to false construction, and the use of constructive parts merely for decoration, and this whether in architecture or in ornament, which is ever dependent upon it. It was this that debased the Gothic in its last period; it was this that reversed the columns of the Tudor style; that broke through pedimental roofings, or placed them unnecessarily within one another; and finally it was the want of even constructive probability that led to the gross extravagances of the Rococo style, and in the characterless age, which has just passed away, crowded our streets with absurdities, and made our architecture a byword and a reproach. Architecture became the mere bond slave of precedents—precedents followed perhaps in the letter but never in the spirit; and thus the mere imitator lorded it over the original thinker. If a church was to be designed, the last consideration of the architect was the arrangement of the general plan, the constructive utility, the comfort and convenience of the people who were to hear and pray, the modes and requirements of the worship that was to be therein celebrated; these were wholly overlooked in order to patch together some Grecian portico and Gothic spire. Or, was a museum to be built, so long as some classic structure could be adapted to the elevation, what care was there concerning the contents that were to be arranged or displayed therein, the convenience for lighting the objects so as to be seen to the best advantage, the best arrangements for visiting them, the provision for future extensions, or the characteristic expression of the whole that was to arise out of all these considerations. How best to stint the various heights within to the diameters and proportions of some oft-reproduced portico was the great question, thus the whole was evolved with the cold frigidity of a dead and classic period, ill adapted to modern wants. From the same causes our theatres looked like prisons so far as any outward character was observed, and our workhouses assumed the jaunty air of cockney palaces.

But if this was the case with our public buildings, it can scarcely be said that our private ones fared better. In our towns, the architect was so hedged in by fiscal regulations, and tied and bound by Acts of Parliament regulating the form, the size, and the number of openings for light and air, the mode of structure, and the very scantlings of his materials,—so watched was he by district surveyors, and so prevented, by all possible means, from any attempt at originality; in consequence of being required to build streets to pattern, with houses all alike within and without, that his imagination was spell-bound, and the new quarters of our towns were necessarily as regular as, and far less striking than, a range of cotton mills. How different this from the vigorous licence of our forefathers, whose picturesque *barbarisms* and careless vigour yet surprise and delight us. What wonder that men who were to design houses to be erected by dozens to the same pattern became so chilled down to the one dead level of unimaginative uniformity, that to fit a plan to some classic elevation from Greece or Rome was the utmost stretch of their inventive powers. Happily, however, these times have passed away, and a new race of architects has arisen with the new order of things.

But while our architects were content to put columns that supported nothing, roofs that covered nothing, and parapets and balustrades that protected nothing; to contrive sham attics to hide the construction of ugly roofs, to make us peep through the scroll-work of a frieze, or the channels of a triglyph instead of a window, or to make the pedestal of a statue into a chimney-pot; how was it likely to fare with furniture, which became a sort of toy architecture? Was it to be wondered at that all constructive shams were increased tenfold when used as ornament? was it surprising that Grecian stone altars formed our sideboards, Roman temples our cabinets, sarcophagi our cellarets and wine coolers, or that our harpsichords stood on lyres instead of legs; that constructive truth, in short, was wholly and entirely disregarded, in order that some favourite type might be reproduced? Was it to be wondered at, moreover, that men broke loose from these dead shams, and, getting sick of these classicalities, entirely deserted constructive truth and symmetrical arrangement; went mad first after Rococoism, and then, in our own days, after picturesque naturalism, and that the very revolution of taste, produced the wildest contradictory faults.

It has already been remarked that true construction includes the proper use of materials; and it might be added that much of what is ornamentally constructive will naturally arise from this source. Thus, how much of beauty in architecture is owing to the arch, at first no doubt a structural necessity, arising out of the impossibility of quarrying blocks of sufficient size to bridge over the wide spaces and intercolumniations of the trabeated system in large buildings. Again, how much beauty is due to the tracery formed by the ribs of groins in Gothic architecture, necessary in themselves to combine lightness with strength. How much also of real character and even of beauty is to be observed in the displayed construction of our old timber houses, with their quarterings and braces, their projecting bays, carved knee timbers, and pierced barge-boards; things apparently tending to an unpromising effect, but when honestly treated, contributing to picturesque beauty and character. So also it might be with our brick buildings—a necessity of our geographical situation on a vast bed of clay, where stone is a costly material—if the material were treated in good faith, and not hidden by the smooth hypocrisy of stucco. How much of life and vivacity might be given to the dull monotony of our streets by the varied interchange of the colour of the bricks, helped perhaps by coloured surface glazings, which would resist damp and smoke, and which, but for the cheap facility of cement, would surely have been perfected long ago.

Our present space will not allow us to enter upon this subject at any length, or it might be fully shown how much that is of importance in "design" is contained in the right use of materials. What is true of stone, of brick, and of wood, is true also of metal. How diverse, for instance, is, or should be, the whole treatment of cast as compared with wrought metal—take forged and cast iron, the lightness and elegance obtainable in the one, contrasted with the necessary solidity and weight of the other: the play of form, fancy, and variety obtainable in wrought iron, now, alas! almost wholly laid aside for the heavy, mechanical, commonplace repetition of cast work. Even in minor constructive operations the true use of materials often evolves the true ornamentation; as for instance, in weaving, as contrasted with printing processes, in basket weaving, &c. &c.

Our age is an age of new materials and new processes, which want carefully considering with a view to evolving from them and for them new and appropriate designs. Gutta-percha and electro-depositing should, equally with iron and glass, have earnest study on the part of the artist, not necessarily to make the former do *cheaply* what wood carving and metal embossing and chasing accomplish, or to bind the latter, when used as building materials, to the five classical orders, but to find the right use of these materials and the decoration *consistent* with that use.

It is worthy of remark that the true novelty of our own time arose almost fortuitously out of the *useful* application of iron and glass treated honestly in construction in the Palace of Crystal of 1851. More earnest study on the part of the artist may be expected to give more artistic combinations, combinations not arrived at by the mere juxtaposition of materials, so often seen in modern buildings.

If there is one rule more than another which may lead us to a style characteristic of our own age, it is that of making the purpose and utility of our buildings or furniture, and every object and utensil the first consideration; then of selecting the proper materials, by the use of which that utility may be most completely obtained; and, thirdly, ornamenting consistently with the nature of the materials chosen, the leading forms arising out of such construction, irrespective of the mere reproduction of the bygone elements and ornamental details of any style. And reverting to what has been already said, that all the great æras of style have been æras of changed construction, it may not be too much to hope that the mighty constructive works of our day, and our changed materials may at last originate some characteristic style, which, impressed with the "mind and body of the time, its form and bearing," may give to the nineteenth century characteristics as strongly marked as those of the eleventh were marked in the ecclesiastical styles which then arose.

CHAPTER IV.

ON UTILITY WHICH MUST BE CONSIDERED BEFORE DECORATION.

THE terms of the third proposition are, that as construction necessarily implies a purpose, utility must precede ornament. In all arts applied to articles for the use, convenience, and comfort of man, from the building which shelters him and the objects of his care, to the meanest utensil which he values enough to desire to render it ornamental, the utility and fitness for intended purpose is, or ought to be, the first consideration. It has been said that design must commence with the choice of the first structural form and the best use of the materials to be employed, and afterwards proceed to the enhancing, enriching, and ornamenting of that utility, or in other words, in accordance with the well-known rule, we must ornament construction, not construct ornament.

This seems an obvious and an almost unnecessary proposition, but it is often completely overlooked; if, however, it were kept prominently in view, it would correct so many grave errors, that it is worth being earnestly enforced and constantly repeated. Thus, with respect to the external structure of both public and private edifices, the errors that arise out of useless constructive ornamentation have already been noticed. Nor are the faults *within* the building, its furniture, its decoration, or its utensils, likely to be less grave, in consequence of the neglect of the principle of the prior claims of utility.

The way in which utility must control decoration is not always so patent as might be inferred, and oftentimes requires most attentive study and research. Thus, after the consideration of the general uses of any building, must come that of its individual apartments, regulating and characterizing the decorative treatment of each; and the hall, the library, the dining and withdrawing room, should each be considered having regard to their separate uses.

What, for instance, can be more practically absurd in a public building, serving as a picture gallery, than to cover the upper part of the halls and ceilings with pictorial subjects, surrounded by gilding and coloured decoration, whose coarse execution, vivid colour and brilliant "entourage," call away the eye from, and quite overpower, the more modest and thoughtful labours of the easel? Would not utility at once suggest that the character of the decorations should be sufficiently grave and simple, quiet and reserved, to support and display, without interfering with these far more valuable works of art? Yet in many of the galleried apartments of the Louvre used for the display of easel pictures, the very reverse of this is the case, and the walls and ceilings are redolent of decorative painting and gilding.

So also, in many of our private houses, you will see those who have spent thousands and tens of thousands on rare and costly works of art, sacrificing them entirely to gaudy wall-papers, manufactured decorations, or glaring carpets. Here *utility* would at once set the inquirer right.

Again, how often do we find cabinets so covered with carved ornaments, that they will not open, so embossed with useless reliefs that it is dangerous to come near them, so heavy that they hide without exhibiting the invaluable rareties they are intended to contain; rich and costly buffets, that have neither sideboard for the dining utensils, nor shelves for displaying the plate, chairs that give no repose to those who sit in them, and caskets that, from being too fragile to be touched, are a misery to their possessors?

There can be no doubt that the cabinet-work of this country is far beyond that of other nations, and that for plain but sound workmanship, including easy action, excellence of framing and joinery, substantiality, and general utility, a chest of drawers, a sideboard, or a table, of English make is unequalled by foreign workmen ; and if not exactly beautiful it is certainly not vulgar. But when beauty is to be added to this utilitarian excellence, we are apt to have "upholsterer's ornament" in the shape of some coarse scroll-work or some Louis Quinze coquillage, originally intended for gilding but rendered heavy, clumsy, absurd, and essentially vulgar by carving it in the same coloured wood as the furniture.

Granted that "design" includes both construction and ornamentation, and that this latter should arise naturally out of the appropriate decoration of suitable materials, we shall arrive, at a law of good taste, which, while it applies to architecture primarily, is equally to be observed in regard to the furniture and fittings which buildings contain, and to the smaller articles of everyday use. If in architecture, for instance, it is false in principle as it is weak in invention to impose on the face of a structure meaningless columns, purposeless porticoes, or useless pediments, it is equally so in furniture to make cabinets, armoires, buffets, or bookcases into miniature temples, with columns which, so far from having anything to support, are moved from under their entablature whenever it is necessary to open a door, and niches equally useless, trenching upon any space which may be devoted to purposes of utility.

Yet in these adaptations, we have, to a certain extent, precedent to guide us, and some sort of architectural rule and lore to refer to. Far more erroneous is the taste when natural imitation is pushed to extremes and the ornaments on a piece of furniture are made to look less like the work of man than nature's own growth, decayed and withered on some old wall or ruined paling. This very idea has in fact occurred to some designers, who have *improved* it into a reality and rendered the stiles and rails of their works into the crumbling wall and broken paling carving on them, by way of enrichment, the brown, shrivelled, and clinging ivy.

It is the merely imitative character of architecture to which we have already alluded, which has so largely contributed to decorative *shams*, to the age of putty, papier-mâché, and gutta-percha. These react upon architecture; and, from the cheapness with which such ornament can be applied and its apparent excellence, the florid and the gaudy takes the place of the simple and the true. A popular writer describes the wearer of cheap finery as having his jewellery "a size larger than anybody else;" and so it is with the cheap finery of imitative ornament: it is always "a size larger" than it should be—bolder, coarser, and more impudent than the true thing; it excites our contempt by its flashy tawdriness, so incongruous with the meanness and vulgarity it is intended to adorn.

From this *manufacture of ornament* arises all that mixture of styles, and that incongruity of parts, which, perhaps, is itself "the style" of this characterless age. Through it, also, the plasterer and the paper-hanger too often usurp the place of the architect, to the certain dismissal of the mason and the wood-carver; and ornament, perchance in itself unobjectionable, is sure in such hands to be grossly misapplied.

The errors to which we have directed attention in our architecture and in our furniture, are equally prevalent in our domestic utensils. The simple forms which were at first evoked by the rudest arts of the potter or the smith, become, as luxury advances, so overladen with superabundant and unnecessary ornament as to render their daily use a constant misery, and their application for domestic purposes a source of continual annoyance to us. Take, for instance, our pottery; here purity of form almost of necessity arises out of constructive utility, and the reliefs governed solely by the imitation of natural objects and not by the requirements of use or the rules of art are quite unsuited to the material; yet how often do we find in porcelain imitative flowers in high relief, glowing and brilliant as the tints of nature, yet looking gaudy as ornaments, and, from their fragile projections, liable to injury from every touch. Even the Dresden may-flower pattern, a production of great beauty on the principle of a diaper of form and colour; in consequence of its minute hollows is quite incapable of being cleansed, and, from the thickness which it adds to the form, contradicts the true effects of porcelain, which should unite lightness with capacity.

A further consideration of the question of design as applied to that division of pottery and porcelain which more especially comprises works of utility, would lead us to assign to constructive form the first attention; and in such works as are intended for vessels of capacity those forms should be adopted which, while they are most elegant, are best fitted for containing or holding. Such articles, moreover, being of continuous use, the power of ready cleansing is of great importance, and should have due attention from the designer. It is to be remembered, also, that the means of receiving that which is to be contained is as necessary as the facility for its ready outpouring; since it is hardly desirable to have to apply a funnel to fill a pitcher or jug intended for constant use, although this may be permitted in a bottle which is required to keep its contents cool, and may have to be carried about, and which is liable to spill the contents by jolting, and therefore needs a smaller aperture. Moreover, a jug, or pitcher, which will admit the hand to cleanse it thoroughly, must be more suited to daily use than one which will not.

A due consideration of utility would regulate the form in many other cases; as, for instance, in cups and other drinking vessels though it might be most graceful to curve the top edge outwards yet, since such a form is likely to overflow the person in drinking, however superior it may be in elegance, it should not be adopted.

When utility is considered before ornament, numerous truths of the like kind will be arrived at, which are entirely overlooked when the order is reversed; thus relief, when used, should be extremely low, and without indented hollows in the composition, as well as without undercuttings, in order to give facility for cleansing; but, while this is required for utility, it is necessary for elegance and beauty also. The Greeks were fully aware of this fact as an important truth, and in their pottery abstained from reliefs, or kept them to the lowest impost: the vases of Etruria have generally their line unbroken by the ornament, and the reliefs on the celebrated Portland vase are so extremely low as entirely to

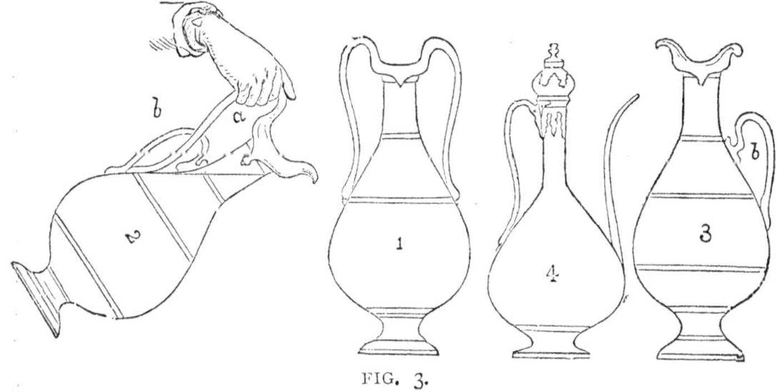

FIG. 3.

preserve its outline. The eastern nations are sensible of the same truth, and their decoration of pottery is on this principle, being entirely subservient to the lines of the form.

The application of handles is another important point connected with constructive design. The easiest and most convenient means of lifting the weight, when lifting only is required, and of lifting and pouring when both are requisite, being the question to be determined. Too often this is arrived at more by chance than by calculation. We see, for instance, the form of an Etruscan vase, such as is shown in Fig. 3, No. 1, adopted as a pitcher; the original having two handles, formed for its occasional removal only; for its new purpose, a spout is substituted for one of the handles; perhaps it is to serve as a ewer, requiring raising and reversing at every effort to pour, and yet, so changed, it is acted upon by the hand and wrist at the greatest possible disadvantage, the hand having to lift the weight, as it were, at the end of a long lever, and reverse it by the power of the wrists, as is shown at *a* (No. 2), while a much less power applied at *b* (Nos. 2 and 3) would suffice to reverse the pitcher and pour forth the fluid. The height of the handle is of less importance when the contents have to be delivered from near the bottom, as in the eastern form at No. 4; since the slightest tilt of the vessel would begin to empty the contents through the spout, which would not be the case if they had to be discharged from the top. These hints will serve to show how important the proper consideration of the insertion of the handles is in such works, and how easily errors arise from merely adopting inconsiderately a form fitted for one use in order to adapt it to another one.

It is also to be remembered that utility may be departed from, and over-ornamentation be produced by a false or excessive use of colour, with which fault so many of our manufactures are chargeable. It does not suffice for true excellence in the case say of woven fabrics, that rare skill is shown in the gradation of the various tints, or rare brilliancy has been obtained in the dyes, or that even the individual pattern has been well and harmoniously arranged. It is the effect of the whole that is to be considered, and its due subordination to the general surroundings and to the position in which it is to be placed. But this will be noticed in the fifth proposition.

CHAPTER V.

ON FITNESS OF THE ORNAMENT TO THE MATERIAL TO WHICH IT IS APPLIED.

WITH regard to the fourth consideration, that "design must be bad which applies the same constructive forms and ornamental treatments indiscriminately to different materials."

It has already been shown that the due ornamentation of construction produces unexpected beauties in architecture, and this is no doubt the case also with those secondary objects of furniture, utensils, and fabrics, which are supplementary to architecture. Moreover, some remarks have been made on the architectural faults arising from the misapplication of decorated constructions to other purposes and materials than those for which they were originally designed.

Each material has its own peculiar constructive qualities; stone those of homogeneity of texture combined with strength, its weight and mass rendering it extremely suitable for arched construction; wood those of continuity of fibre, and strength conjoined with lightness, rendering it available for bridging over wide spaces, and from the direction of its fibre necessitating right-lined rather than circular or arched construction; metal those of strength due to tenacity of fibre, combined with a large amount of homogeneity rendering it equally fitted with wood for crossing wide spaces, with less bulk of material in proportion to weight than either wood or stone, and fitting it by its tenacity, for either right-lined or curved constructive forms.

With reference to the decoration of these several materials, the homogeneity of grain in the stone, and its perfect freedom under the tool, admirably adapt it for carving, but necessitate a different treatment to that for the continuous fibre of wood. The latter will bear more finesse of execution than the former, and a more detached relief; the colour, as light or dark, or veined and mottled, the hardness or softness, the intractibility or freedom of the grain in wood, moreover, require peculiar renderings of the ornament; while metal, whether the ornament be cast, chased, or embossed, evidently demands a totally different treatment to either.

Again, the position of the ornament requires special consideration, as, for instance, its height above the ground, or point of view, which will govern both its relief and execution: while much more varied quantities, bolder relief, and coarser execution are not only allowable but absolutely necessary at heights considerably above the eye.

The practice of cutting the ornament after the stone has been placed in the structure, so universal with the best Gothic carvers in mediæval times,* and still practised by the French workmen, admits of a right estimate of the true relief and just quantity of ornament, but from this very circumstance (its relation to situation,) the mere reproduction of such ornament is often very unsatisfactory; for it must be remembered that the fitness of ornament for its special situation, and for the peculiar material in which it was to be wrought, was a necessity in its first production, but is overlooked in its mere imitative repetition.

If then the translation of ornament, even from one position to another, requires that it should be greatly modified and changed,

* An instance of this may be seen in one of the west towers of Rouen Cathedral :—the stone is built into the structure with the requisite projections, but much of the carving has never been completed.

still more so is this the case when the material in which it is to be wrought is changed also.

The heavy scroll-work of a Roman frieze carved in stone, although appropriate in its place far above the eye, must be quite unsuitable carved in wood as the back of a sideboard, and still more so, cast in iron as part of a gate or a balcony, where it is not only close to the eye, but pierced through between the foliage, which in the original was backed out and supported by the ground from which it was carved. Still more absurd is this same scroll-work imitated in relief on a carpet or tablecloth, or a muslin curtain. Yet such anomalies are continually occurring, arising perhaps from the use of casts of antique ornament as a means of study; their beauty becomes so impressed upon our minds that it is hard to appreciate fully their unsuitableness for every purpose.

In this respect, indeed, originality is less to be hoped for in each succeeding age. As a writer is sure imperceptibly to reproduce something of the books he has read, so the artist cannot entirely forget those works through which his studies have been conducted. The path to excellence may be shortened, but other minds have set up their landmarks upon it. Thus studying art, as we must do, in and through art, nature is apt to be overlooked, propriety to be neglected, and fitness to be disregarded, and all that we do is liable to become more or less a varied repetition of what has been done before.

Moreover, each fabric and each material has its peculiar texture, lustre, &c., and even when the uses are the same the translation of ornament from one fabric to another is rarely successful and is often productive of very bad taste. Thus in the case of woven hangings, what might be suitable and beautiful in silk would be dull and heavy in worsted, and coarse and extravagant in muslin. The same holds good in garment fabrics also, where forms that may be unobjectionable in silk of a self colour would be large and extravagant in varied colours, and utterly tasteless in a printed de laine. Thus ornament must be studied for the special material it is to be wrought in, or however agreeable it may be when seen on paper as a design, it will be found to be in bad taste when it is executed.

Again, each mode of execution has its characteristic qualities, and each produces its own peculiar and varied beauties, and thus requires its special application of ornament. It is one of the difficulties of manufacture, to render by the machine and in the particular material to be used, all that the mind and hand has shown in the design, or to indicate in the design all that the material will add to it of lustre, beauty, or richness. Again it is a matter of extreme difficulty and one requiring long experience in manufacture, to tell how a design will work; and connected with this difficulty is the due appreciation of the changes that must take place in the translation of the design from the paper to the fabric to produce the effect sought for. Nor does the consideration end here. There is still the difficulty which remains to the purchaser, and requires an effort of judgment, which many are wholly incapable of exercising: viz., the power to know how the decoration of the material will appear in use. Thus a garment fabric may be beautiful in itself, but look ill when made up for wear, and a silk hanging or a paper hanging which we admire in the pattern may, and often does, disappoint us extremely when it is hung; and this supports a former remark on the appropriateness of ornament being governed in some respects by position as well as material.

As the lustre and brilliancy of silk must be considered in its ornamentation, the material itself lending so much beauty to the design wrought in it, so there are many other cases wherein the material has a rare beauty, which must be preserved, sometimes arising from its purity and translucency, as in the case of glass and white marble, sometimes from its colour, as in ivory, sometimes from its beauty and purity of surface, as in porcelain. Thus, as it would not be desirable to paint marble or to stain ivory, neither is it desirable to destroy the whole surface of porcelain by decoration, however rich or however beautiful.

In no other branch of our manufactures perhaps is the fitness of the ornament to the material so much disregarded as in metal work, and more particularly in the characteristic and marked differences which should arise in the proper treatment of wrought in distinction to cast metal.

CHAPTER VI.

ON UNITY OF STYLE AND DECORATIVE SUBORDINATION.

We have yet to consider that unity of style and proper subordination of one work to another, and to the whole external and internal decoration, which is so necessary to true taste.

It has already been said that there must be some predominating influence, some prevailing sentiment present in the minds of men to produce a style. Did this influence really exist, it would be seen in all that a man possessed, and a certain unity of character in his house and all his belongings would be the necessary result.

In the mediæval times this predominating sentiment was the respect of the many to the outward forms of a material religion; thus the aspect of all that a man possessed was ecclesiastical—his furniture carved with emblems of the church, and his walls covered with the choice precepts of religion—as in the times of Judaism, when in the same spirit of outward respect the Pharisees wore the holy texts on the frontlets of their brows, and wove precepts, which they ought to have acted upon, into the borders of their garments.

In our own times any wide-spread sentiment is unfortunately wanting, and the greater number of even wealthy people are content to live in dwellings and to be surrounded with furniture totally incongruous in character the one with the other. This being the case, additions are made from time to time with the same careless indifference as to the harmony of the whole : each work is purchased for itself alone, with little reference to others, either as to style, to colour, or to relative subordination in decorative richness, till the house is like a museum, and the taste of the possessor being more and more vitiated and vulgarised, it becomes hard to impress him with any belief in the beauty which would result, not from uniformity, but from the mere absence of incongruity.

It may be objected that the principle of unity or congruity, however observable in the mediæval period, was never attended to by the great artists of the renaissance, and that we continually see in their works and in their additions to other works, the strangest inconsistencies and anomalies. This is perfectly true, but it most probably arose from reasons quite apart from their rejection or recognition of the justice of the principle.

These revivalists, coming with all the ardent enthusiasm of converts from the study of classic art, and convinced in their own minds of its ideal perfection and beauty, found the land covered with vast and magnificent temples and structures, deep in the love and reverence of what they deemed the *vulgar* public, and venerable from age and from consecration to God, yet of a style and character wholly opposed to the one they sought to introduce. The reconstruction of these time-honoured edifices was hopeless, and the new race of architects began to seize upon and *adorn* the *interiors* of the old cathedrals and churches of Europe with rood-screens, stalls, altars, confessionals, pulpits, and monuments, in the new style of the renaissance, quite irrespective of the character of the original structure. In process of time they even ventured to make additions to the very structure itself. Thus, in our own country, Inigo Jones, not foreseeing the fiery purgation that was to prepare the way for the great monument of the new art, did not hesitate to build a classic portico to the Gothic structure of old St. Paul's; and it is impossible to enter the churches and cathedrals of France and Belgium without seeing how continuous was the endeavour to seduce the people gradually into the new faith in art, by additions such as those we have spoken of above.

The apostles of the renaissance did, in fact, but follow the practice and example of the early missionaries of Roman Christianity. These sought to humour the superstitions of the Pagan worshippers, and to wile them into truth by adopting, not only their festivals and holidays, but also their temples and altars, consecrating them to the new faith, and at the same time smoothing down those distinctive differences that were most repugnant to their old belief. In our own day, and following out the same course of action, an eloquent writer on art proposes to revert to what he considers the sounder taste of our Gothic forefathers, by making piecemeal additions and alterations to our houses, and patching their bald and characterless horizontalism with gazebos and porches of a mediæval character.

As was the result in respect to Christianity, where a like practice propagated all sorts of errors and superstitions, whose parasitical growth nearly strangled the parent plant, so the various compromises and adaptations which architects thought reasonable in reviving classic art, have been the source of errors which have grown up side by side with the new style, and by their grotesque absurdity marred the beauty with which they had common birth.*

The Gothic principle of progress in style was essentially different from that of the renaissance. New and increased enrichment invariably began in the interior of the building, in the shrines, altar-screens, stalls, and monuments of churches, and the

* Even the faults and absurdities which were thus admitted are now so hallowed by time, and moreover offer such marked characteristics and illustrations of the age that produced them, that one would hesitate to suggest their removal, however much we may object to them as errors, and protest against their reproduction. There can be but little doubt that the florid classic altars, the chubby, cloud-borne cherubs, with their gilt palm branches, however incongruous with a Gothic cathedral, as truly exemplify the pretentious age of Louis le Grand, and the preaching of Bossuet, Bourdaloue, and Fénelon, as the writings and sermons addressed to it which these authors have left behind them.

furniture and utensils of private dwellings (more particularly in the former however, as the style was essentially ecclesiastical), and gradually these enrichments passed from within the building, from its enshrinements as it were, to the decoration of the outside of the building itself. In the renaissance, on the contrary, as has just been shown, the constructive ornamentation of the exterior of the building became the model of the interior furniture and fittings, and hence arose many of the faults that have been already pointed out.

It is in the nature of imitators to seize on the most salient points, whether good or bad, and to exaggerate them; in the same way that a tasteless portrait painter caricatures a feature or expression in order to give a coarse and telling likeness. So the more recondite beauties of the renaissance, those which appeal to the highest minds, have been overlooked, and the grotesque and the novel features have been considered as the elements of the style, disregarding much in it that was spiritual and refined. This very incongruity, a fault, perhaps a necessary one at the period of the revival, has been thus perpetuated as a beauty, while it is in reality an error and a mistake; for unity of style and decorative subordination are indispensable to true taste; all admit this in a degree, since none trust completely to indiscriminate selection. Most people allow a subordination in the apartments of the houses, and do not decorate the hall, the library, or the dining-room so richly as the drawing-room or the boudoir. Moreover, there is usually some desire, often, it is true, with little knowledge, to have a due subordination in colour also in the furniture of individual apartments, and an effort is at least made that the carpets, the hangings, and the walls should have some harmonious agreement.

Is it too much then to assert that there should be a subordination as to uses also, and that the carpets and the wall-papers should be subdued and quiet, as forming the background of the apartment; while the chairs and tables, the cabinets and commodes, the mirrors and picture-frames should each have such an amount of decoration, and only such, as is justly relative to their importance to the whole?

If this is true of furniture collectively considered, it is true also irrespective of this condition, and many of the gross errors, and much of the useless and improper expenditure, evident in all sections of our manufactures, would be avoided by proper attention to this rule.

If also the previous arguments are correct, it will be seen that the authority of antiquity in its best periods, the authority of Nature as displayed in her works, the natural laws of form and colour, as well as the conditions and limitations of manufactures and the purposes of utility, are in favour of some such principles of decorative design as those which have been laid down.

One reason for the prevalence of so much lawlessness and absence of correct principles in our manufactures is due to the fact that the law of pictorial art prevails rather than the law of ornamental art. Now, although the office of a picture is to bring some object, some incident, some history or subject to the eye of the spectator, and to touch and please him with the passion, sentiment, or feeling which it is fitted to instil, it does this quite irrespective of the material in which or on which it is wrought. What have the canvas, the paper, the mere copper, or the panel to do with the enjoyment of a work of fine art? But ornament, on the contrary, if what has been said is in any degree correct, cannot be dissevered from the material, from which indeed much of its varied effect arises; and the character of the decoration adopted should be in accordance with the material, and with the uses of the object decorated. So much so ought this to be the case, that it might be expected, that to see the design, or even a careful description of the ornament, would be sufficient to enable us to determine the nature and the uses of the object itself.

END OF SECTION I.

SECTION II.

THE APPLICATION OF THE PRINCIPLES OF ORNAMENT TO THE MANUFACTURES.

CHAPTER VII.

ON THE NATURE AND GENERAL APPLICATION OF ORNAMENTAL ART.

The desire evinced by the rudest, as well as the most civilized nations for the decoration of their buildings, utensils, and clothing almost raises ornament into a natural want, and must render its proper application of the utmost consequence to the manufacturer, since upon it the value of his manufactures in the various markets of the world chiefly depends. Whether we regard the war-club and the paddle of the savage, or the priceless jewel of Cellini; the simple woven matwork of the South Sea islander, or the gorgeous masterpiece of the Utrecht loom, we find that the ornament in every case has been governed in its application by certain definite rules or principles, and these principles we have endeavoured to formulate in the foregoing chapters. By some such well-defined laws all design and all decoration must be judged, and it is only by a careful study of the best works of all periods, and an earnest search after what is found to be good and true in the art of each people and each period that we can devise rules for the guidance and instruction of the designer.

In our opening chapters we have endeavoured to gather some of the principles which should govern the application of ornament, and before we proceed to apply these principles to the various branches of our manufactures, we may glance briefly at the nature of ornament and the conditions of its employment in the arts and manufactures.

We have spoken of design and of ornamental decoration. These are two essentially different things, and it is highly necessary that they should, from the first, be considered as separate and distinct. "Design" has reference to the construction of any work both for use and beauty, and therefore includes its ornamentation also. "Ornament" on the other hand implies merely the decoration of an object already constructed.

Ornament is thus necessarily limited, for, so defined, it cannot be other than secondary, and must not usurp a principal place; if it do so, the object is no longer a work ornamented, but is degraded into a mere *ornament.* The tendency too much of the present time is, as we have already shown, to reverse this state of things, to the utter subversion of all true principles of taste.

The ornament of past ages is the *tradition* of the ornamentist, and tradition ever hands down to us things both good and bad, each equally consecrated to most minds by the authority of antiquity. But a moment's reflection will show how necessary it is to discriminate before receiving anything on such authority. A church or temple built in a rude age remains undisturbed by some happy chance, a villa or a theatre in a remote provincial town escapes the fatalities of accident or time, some tomb is opened, some overwhelmed city exhumed from the *débris* of ruin that had gathered over it. The ornamental details found therein are copied and illustrated by the notes of the antiquarian, or published in the proceedings of learned societies, and are at once regarded as authorities for imitation, forgetting all the while that they may have been perhaps the works of obscure provincial artists, of a barbarous age perchance, or of a people among whom *art,* no longer studied for its principles, had ceased to progress or had rapidly declined.

Such traditional ornament moreover had or had not a local use, a consistent application to domestic, ecclesiastical, or funeral purposes, in fact a local symbolism; but whether it had such or not (a fact mostly overlooked) is sure to be soon disregarded; and not only have we ornament of a degraded period, of a declining age, or by inferior artists, but to this must be added, one whose symbolic life is totally extinct, and, perhaps, fortunately so, for when revived it is indiscriminately used, for purposes totally at variance with its first application and original intent.

Ornamentists may fairly be divided into two classes: the traditional, who superstitiously reverence the remains of past ages and are wedded in practice to existing styles; and those who despise the past and feel themselves at liberty to adopt from the abundant sources of nature a mode and manner for themselves, without regard to the works of their predecessors. The first class desire simply to follow where precedent leads them, and to be able to claim the sanction of authority for their works. These, even when taste duly regulates their choice, are men of limited ideas and small progress. Those of the second class, who pay no deference to authority, who think that ornament is governed by no laws, and who recognise no principles by which they are to be guided, are little likely to raise the art to the level of past times, and, still less are they likely to advance its aim and widen its scope. The true ornamentist would seem to be one who seeks out the *principles* on which the bygone artists worked, and the rules by which they arrived at excellence, and, discarding mere imitation and reproduction of details, endeavours, by the application of new ideas and new matter upon *principles* which he believes to be sound, or which time and the assent of other minds has approved to be fundamental, to attain originality through fitness and truth. The antiquarian ornamentist, however, will always have a certain reputation, and justly too if he has the taste to select what is best from the great masters of past times. In any case the critic must be bold who speaks against the authority of the fathers of the art; and praise is safe when great names are on the critic's side. From this latter class of ornamentists we may at least demand purity of style, we may require that marked æras should be kept distinct, and that the adopted ornament should be fitly applied to fabrics or manufactures of the like nature, and, as far as possible, for the like uses, as those for which the ornament was first designed.

From the labours of the second class of ornamentists, united to that constant search after novelty at any sacrifice of true taste for which manufacturers are so constantly urgent, there has arisen a new species of ornament of the most objectionable kind, which we cannot too strongly deprecate on account of its complete departure from just taste and true principles. This to which we have already alluded may be called the *natural* or merely imitative style, and it is seen in its worst development in some of the articles of form.

Thus we have metal *imitations* of plants and flowers, with an attempt to make them a strict resemblance, forgetting that natural objects are rendered into ornament by subordinating the details to the general idea, and that the endeavour ought to be to seize the simplest expression of a thing rather than to imitate the thing itself. This is the case with fine art also, in every phase of which, mere imitation is an error and an impertinence; and true ornamental art is even more opposed to the merely imitative treatment now so largely adopted. Let any one examine floral or foliated ornament produced in metal by electrotyping the natural object, whereby every venation and striation of the plant is reproduced, and compare it with a well and simply modelled treatment, where only the general features of the form are given and all the more minute details purposely omitted; and if this latter has been done with a true sense of the characteristics of the plant, the meanness and littleness of the one mode will be perfectly evident, compared with the larger manner of the other. But this imitative style is carried much further: or-molu stems and leaves bear porcelain flowers painted to imitate nature, and candles are made to rise out of tulips and china-asters, while gas jets gush forth from opal arums. Stems, bearing flowers for various uses, arise from groups of metal leaves standing painfully on their points, and every constructive truth, and just adaptation to use, is sacrificed for a senseless imitative naturalism. In the same way, and doubtless supported by great authorities, past and present, enormous wreaths of flowers, fish, game, fruits, &c., imitated *à merveille*, dangle round sideboards, beds, and picture-frames. Glass is tortured out of its true quality to make it into the cup of a lily or an anemone : not that we may be supposed to drink nectar from the flower, but that the novelty may catch those for whom good taste is not piquant enough, and for whom chaste forms are not sufficiently showy. In fabrics where flatness would seem most essential, this imitative treatment is often carried to the greatest excess ; and carpets are ornamented with water-lilies floating on their natural bed, with fruits and flowers poured forth in overwhelming abundance in all the glory of their hues and shades ; or we are startled by a lion at our hearth, or a leopard on our rug, his spotted coat imitated even to its relief as well as in its colour, while palm-trees and landscapes are used as the ornaments of muslin curtains. Though far from saying that imitative ornament is not sometimes allowable, still it will at once be felt that the manner of its use wants a determined regulation to exclude it in most of the above-mentioned cases from all works aspiring to be considered in just taste, and to leave it to be adopted by those only who think novelty better than chaste design, and who consider that display is preferable to truth.

The constant search after novelty has just been alluded to as one of the sources of bad taste in modern adornment. Manufacturers are eager to obtain it at any sacrifice of truth, and at any cost. The efforts of those past ages, when taste was most indisputable, appear, as we have already shown, to have been directed rather to the continually perfecting and refining their designs and inventions, than to creating new ones. Thus in architecture the robust simplicity and grandeur of the Doric order remained unchanged from generation to generation, the only discernible effort being to perfect just proportions and true symmetry of parts, rather than to add any novelty of feature or ornament, until, in the Parthenon, it seems to have arrived at the most perfect development that taste, science, and art could unitedly effect: even among the more voluptuous inhabitants of Asia Minor, at least until the age when their artists became servants and panderers to the coarser magnificence of Rome, the details of ornamentation were few, and those universally received. The volute, the acanthus, the anthemion, the æchinus, and a few frets and guilloches, seemed to pass the ordeal of criticism, not that they might be rejected for more novel treatments, but that the symmetry of their parts might be more justly balanced, the commoner curves rejected for those more varied, beautiful, and refined, and the true impost given to their projections. Proportion and symmetry being thus sought after instead of novelty, Grecian ornament has come down to us with authority like that of Scripture, rather than of tradition, and all the after efforts of artists, who have adopted and adapted it, have failed either to improve its elegance, or to add to its beauty. In the eastern nations we find the same usage prevail, and to this day Indian ornament is composed of the same forms as it was in the earliest known works: the principles that governed ornamental practice in those works seem still to be a tradition with the artist and the workman, and still to produce the same beautiful results, as is abundantly seen in the fabrics and tissues of modern Indian workmanship. Now, however, our efforts are of an entirely different nature, and the hunger after novelty is quite insatiable; heaven and earth are racked for novel inventions, and happy is the man who lights upon something, however *outré*, that shall strike the vulgar mind, and obtain the "run of the season." Such patterns result as often from the caprice of accident as from any effort of thought—witness what was called the diorama pattern in cotton-printing, once very popular, which was the result of an accidental folding of the stuff on the cylinder in printing. Accepted for the season, these fantasies no sooner pass away than the world wonders how it could ever have looked upon them with satisfaction, or tolerated for an instant such solecisms in taste, such strange incongruities, or such gross absurdities.

The ornament of past ages was chiefly the offspring of handicraft labour, that of the present age is the child of the engine and the machine. This great difference in the mode of production causes a like difference in the results. In old times the artist was at once designer, ornamentist, and craftsman, and to him was indifferent the use of the pencil or the brush, of the hammer, the chisel, or the punch : his hand and his mind wrought together, not only in the design, but in every stage of its completion, and thus there entered a portion of that mind into every minute detail, and into every stage of finish, and many a beautiful after-thought was embodied by the hand of the "cunning artificer," many a grace added to the work by his mastery and skill. He worked, not to produce a rigid sameness, but he worked as Nature works : —she produces nothing exactly similar to its fellow ; in every turn of every stage of growth, in every flower, and in every leaf, adding a changing grace, a differing beauty ; so he varied his labours with every feeling of his overflowing mind. But this is not possible with the stamp, the mould, the press, and the die, the ornamental agents of our days : after the type or model is made, all the products are rigidly the same, whence arises a tiresome sameness, a sickening monotony, unknown in the works of nature and peculiar to these artificial works of man : the varying mind has no share in their production, and man himself becomes only the servant of the machine.

Moreover, the old ornamentist worked generally from feelings of piety, from love of his labours, or from the desire for fame, motives hardly known to the artist of this class in our days, at least in this country—Who seeks fame from the ephemera of a season ? Who loves a labour that is so soon to pass away ? Who cares for a work that is not to be the child of his own hand, but to be produced in thousands by the aid of machinery? The toil of the artificer of olden times was spent upon the thing itself, and not upon a mere model for it: the chalice, the cup, the lock and key, or the reliquary, were to be without repetition, and without rivals: he sought to give them their highest excellence, and, labouring from one of the feelings we have described, threw his whole soul into his work, so that it became a thing for future ages to look upon and to prize. Not that handicraft or art-workmanship is utterly excluded from our manufactures; it is only partially so, making it all the more painfully evident how greatly ornamental art has suffered from its new union with machinery. Wherever ornament is wholly effected by machinery, it is certainly the most degraded in style and execution; and the best workmanship and the best taste is invariably to be found in those manufactures and fabrics wherein handicraft is entirely or partially the means of producing the ornament, as in china and glass, in works in the precious metals, carving, &c. These faults arise partly from the facilities which machinery gives to the manufacturer, enabling him to produce the florid and over-loaded as cheaply as the simple forms, and thus to satisfy the larger market for the multitude, who desire quantity rather than quality, and value a thing the more, the more it is ornamented. This state of modern manufacture, whereby ornament is multiplied without limit from a given model, by the machine or the mould, ought at least to awaken in the manufacturer a sense of the importance of the first design. One would think that what was to be produced by thousands and tens of thousands should at any rate be a work of beauty, and that no pains would be spared to insure its excellence. The cost of the first design or model must in such a case be a mere atom when divided among its myriad reproductions. It would seem strange, however, to judge by the results, in some cases, that any one could be found to throw away great expense upon dies and moulds, to carry out a design which in itself was hardly thought worth paying for. Yet often in this country artists are paid little better than workmen, and a belief seems to prevail, that knowledge, skill, and taste come by nature : the artist has seldom any interest in the result of his labours, his name is unknown, his pay is niggardly, and what there may be of beauty and excellence in his work is often spoiled by the alterations of the manufacturer, who makes no scruple of setting his own taste above that of the artist, and altering and changing a design at his sole pleasure.

In France, and in some parts of Germany, where taste has long been cultivated, and the value of ornamental design is better appreciated, these relations are better understood also; and in this country, if good taste is to prevail, the manufacturer must learn to appreciate more highly the value of the designer's labours, must seek to foster his talents and stimulate his *amour propre* by giving him some increased share in his successful endeavours. Society also must be prepared to contribute more largely than heretofore to public education in ornamental art, and taste must be disseminated by every available means ; for it is not only a truth, but a truth that should everywhere be told, that, notwithstanding our skilful workmanship and our excellence in the manufacture of most fabrics, we have been until quite lately sadly behind-hand in the design applied to them, and greatly indebted to foreign artists even for what little that was good.

Moreover, our greatest difficulty consists even less in the want of designers than of skilled art-workmen to carry out designs. A design for cotton-printing may be spoiled by the "putter-on," or for silk by him who prepares it for the loom. The sculptor may design a statuette, but there are few able to chase the bronze, to retouch the clay, or to unite the parts when they come forth from the mould. Even where such are found, they are mostly men of slow minds, who enter little into the spirit of the artist's labours, and who work without feeling as without fire. We find plenty of chasers able to imitate the fur of animals, or the texture of draperies, but few who understand the bones and the anatomy of the parts, and fewer still who carry an artist's spirit into their works. In decorative painting, also, the painter on glass and china is generally a mere copyist, or he works too entirely by rote, and without feeling. The lily and the rose which he paints are always the same lily and the same rose, a work of the hand and eye, in which the mind has no share. There are honourable exceptions, no doubt, but with the many art is a mere handicraft, partaking only in the smallest degree of those higher qualities which, as we have seen, animated the art-workmen of mediæval times, and prior to the introduction of machinery. One of the best tendencies of the present age, and also the one holding out the best promises for the future, is a desire in some manufactures to return to the typical forms of hand-worked ornament, and to bring into its due prominence the superior value of honestly hand-wrought decoration.

CHAPTER VIII.

ON THE DECORATION OF BUILDINGS.

HAVING in our last chapter glanced at the general nature of ornament, we may now proceed to the second division of our subject, viz., the application of the principles formulated in our first section to the different branches of our manufactures. It will be advisable for facility of reference to classify the subject under four general heads :—Decoration of Buildings—Domestic and other Furniture —Domestic Utensils and Objects of Personal Use—Garment Fabrics.

These general heads may again be subdivided as follows :—

1. Decoration of buildings, consisting of—

   1st. Architectural decoration, painted, &c.
   2nd. Stone, carved wood, terra cotta, carton-pierre, and other relief decorations.
   3rd. Stained glass.
   4th. Inlaid floors, mosaic pavement, inlaid tiles, &c.
   5th. Paper and other hangings.
   6th. Metal-work.

2. Domestic and other furniture, including cabinet-work of all kinds, and furniture of all materials.

   1st. Cabinets, sideboards, and furniture generally.
   2nd. Stoves, grates, fenders, lamps, gas-fittings, and other hardware.
   3rd. Carpets, portières, table-covers, and floor-cloths.
   4th. Curtains and hangings.
   5th. Table-linen.

3. Domestic utensils and objects of personal use.

    1st. Porcelain, pottery, &c.
    2nd. Table and ornamental glass.
    3rd. Works in the precious metals and jewellery, clocks, &c.
    4th. Bookbinding.

4. Garment fabrics.

    1st. Woven in patterns of any material, and hand-worked.
    2nd. Printed.
    3rd. Lace.
    4th. Ribbons.

In reviewing these classes we shall endeavour under each of the above headings to point out the more salient defects arising from the introduction of false principles; selecting here and there a few good examples for the sake of illustrating our meaning, and showing more clearly what we have to expect when correct and true principles have been followed.

We may now pass on to the consideration of our first group:— THE DECORATION OF BUILDINGS. Properly speaking, the design for the decoration of any building, both externally and internally, is the province of its architect, since in this case decoration is essentially a part of architecture. If the principle we have before enunciated, that ornament is the decoration of construction, be just, it will be apparent that it is hardly possible to judge of the one without the other. In works wherein the decorator makes his own sham construction in order to ornament it, as well as in those multiplied manufactured "parts" which form the staple ornament of a large class of workmen in this line, we may admire the skill of the execution, the cleverness of the details, the excellence of the manufacture, or the imitation of early works of acknowledged merit; but to appreciate "decoration" we must view it as a whole in the place for which it was specially designed, and in harmony with the building whose construction it ornaments. Moreover, it must mainly originate in local circumstances, and ought to have an individual significance. In this respect we soon become sensible how impracticable it is to lay down any general rules for our guidance under the singular complications of modern house decoration.

Papier-mâché, carton-pierre, and a host of other cheap modes of ornamentation, have no doubt a substantial value commercially considered. As regards design, however, they are but dangerous subsidiaries, often doing more injury than good, owing to the tasteless, misplaced, and false decoration arising from their use. Apart from that monotonous multiplication of the same forms, necessarily resulting from the unvarying productions of the mould and the die, which has been before alluded to, there are other evils sure to accompany *manufactured* decorations such as those now under consideration. The great cheapness of the substitute, compared with the real material, inevitably leads to excess. Such ornament always seems added or applied, stuck on as it were, and can rarely be made to appear as a part of construction; it therefore constantly carries with it a sense of untruth, till the mind and eye, from habit, become satisfied with it, and at the same time deadened to what is really true and good.

Moreover, decoration consisting of such materials must necessarily always be patchy and incomplete. When the parts to be ornamented are large, this evil is seen in its most exaggerated form; a florid and gaudy centre has perhaps to be united with coarse corners, either by other ornaments or by the repetition of the centre portion, and all sorts of expedients must be resorted to, to "bring in" the parts so as to suit the architectural distribution of the apartment; it can indeed barely be possible that the quantities, or the geometrical arrangement in which the ornament has been originally constructed, will agree with the place to which it has to be adapted, and more or less of make-shift must be the result.

The whole system of modern house-finishing, so far as regards the *appliqué* work of the plasterer and the decorator, is utterly false and untrue. A cornice so many inches in depth is found to be needed, and from a well-filled storehouse of such works in every style the plasterer, disregarding every other consideration, seeks the pattern which most readily complies with the necessary conditions of depth and projection. A centre-flower for the ceiling so many feet in diameter is the next requisite, and, the labours of the plasterer at an end, the decorator and the upholsterer step in, and the former touches up his work with colour applied with no regard to relative fitness and appropriate gradation, while the upholsterer sends in the hangings and furniture suited to another country and another age. Scale seems to have been quite disregarded in the work of the plasterer, since the fruit and flowers, the birds and game, of one part, are different in size from those of another part. The style, again, is mixed, one part being two centuries earlier than the other. There is, besides, far more pains taken with the exact rendering of fur or a feather, than in perfecting the form of a moulding, or the shape of a panel—the architecture has, in the designer's mind, been subordinate to the ornament, and an ill-formed ellipse, or a coarse and unrefined moulding, appears of less importance to him than the mere imitation of the feathers of his birds, or the fur of the animals of which his ornament consists. Carry this treatment a little further, and it will result in having the game, the fruit, the foliage, and the flowers not only modelled to the exactest imitation, but the skill of the painter called in to add to its naturalism, and the whole painted with the colours of nature; thus decoration will be thought perfect only when it competes with those strange groups in relief we sometimes find framed to form a picture.

One great cause of evil in the use of the materials under consideration consists in the false principle of their application to decorative purposes. It is found, for instance, that peculiar qualities, which are difficult of attainment and an effort of great skill in other materials, can easily be obtained by a new means; instead, therefore, of carefully studying its just adaptation to ornamental production, the effort is only to emulate in excess of skill those peculiar qualities which are trials in the more intractable material.

It too often happens, moreover, that the original works imitated were in false taste; and this becomes far more apparent in the copies, since the mind can no longer dwell on them with that admiration which is caused by a sense of difficulties overcome, and which compensated, in some degree, for the absence of good taste in the works they emulate. As instances the exact imitation in wood or stone carving of the individual details rather than of the general character of objects used as ornament, extreme relief, under-cutting, lightness, thinness, and picturesqueness of the forms of foliage and flowers, whereby their natural growth is attempted in carving rather than a due ornamental disposition of their forms—all tending to excess and exaggeration, and to be avoided rather than copied.

Another source of error consists in rendering what should be true constructive forms into mere ornament; thus pilasters, and even columns, consoles and trusses intended to support weight, are manufactured in these imitative materials, and introduced only to decorate, until all sense of utility and construction is lost, and ornament becomes the principal instead of the subordinate.

During the past few years there has been a marked revival in the use of terra cotta for structural purposes, and there are numerous signs in the buildings recently erected and still in progress in many parts of the metropolis that its proper treatment as a material for ornamentation is becoming appreciated by our architects. As an enrichment for brick buildings there can be no fitter material, and from the fact that, although it at first originates from the mechanical process of moulding, terra cotta admits of any amount of subsequent perfecting by hand, there are few materials more deserving of careful and considerate treatment. The points to be regarded are chiefly these:—First, to beware of a stone treatment or the attempt which so many terra cotta manufacturers have always before their eyes of making terra cotta a substitute for stone; and second, to remember that, as it has to be produced in numberless repetitions from a mould, the ornament should be in low relief and free from undercutting. The above observations apply of course to terra cotta as a material to be used in construction. It has for very many years occupied a prominent position for the manufacture of decorative objects for our gardens and suburban villas. The constructive forms of many of such works are, it is true, to be traced back to the antique, but so vulgarised in proportion and in their curves, as to be wholly spoilt. The ornamentation moreover of these forms is, as a rule, too redundant; the material is so pliant under the manipulation of the modeller, lends itself so readily to ornament, admits so easily of additional details, that, unless in the hands of a true artist, over-ornamentation is sure to result. One great rule for such works is that beauty of form should first be sought for, and then that the leading lines should be sparingly decorated.

STAINED GLASS DECORATION.

The art of painting on glass, or glass-staining, has come down to us so intimately mixed up with the ecclesiastical architecture of the middle ages, that it is almost impossible to view the one unconnected with the other. It was born of the same parent (the Church), and from the first both were equally devoted to her service. Of Gothic architecture, and of it almost exclusively, stained glass has always formed a necessary decoration: it follows, therefore, that its ornamentation is almost wholly traditional, and has relation to the various periods of the Gothic architecture which it accompanies.

Not that it is necessary, or even desirable, that the epochs of the two arts should, in their revival, continue to correspond; but the periods of each, whether simultaneous or otherwise, when utility and beauty were most fully understood and attained, should be diligently studied in search of the principles that guided the artists of those times, and that which is best should be chosen, irrespective of mere correspondence of epoch or antiquarian authority. Moreover the errors, which the ignorance of an early age evidently occasioned, should be carefully separated from the truths, and not considered as of necessity a part of the *style* of the period in which they are found,—such, more particularly, as bad drawing and want of knowledge of the human figure ; at the same time, that simplicity of treatment which is so highly characteristic of early works, which overlooks all details, and renders a composition from the Scriptures, or a single figure, more as a symbol than as a picture, should, as a principle of excellence, be carefully retained.

As is the case with all other manufactures and fabrics, so it is with painted glass : the question of utility, rightly considered, will lead us to some knowledge of what is most suitable in its treatment as a decoration. Glass was introduced into the numerous windows of Gothic architecture to temper the glare of light, and to serve in a manner as a blind by preventing the direct entrance of the sun's rays, and also to shed that solemn religious light which so well accords with the sacred mysteries of religious worship. The mosaic glass of the early artists of the 12th and 13th centuries was most admirably adapted for this purpose : being composed of many small pieces of full and pure tints, with little white glass, the rays of the sun were broken and dispersed, the light was lowered in brilliancy, and the whole effect was homogeneous, rich, and solemn ; sufficient light being still permitted to enter for the performance of the religious services of the church. Even compositions of figures were subject to the principle that regulated the whole : the figures were small, so that the colour of their draperies and accessories might be broken up into many pieces to give the same equal distribution as in the ornamental parts of the window. It would seem, indeed, that the painter did not intend to simulate a picture, but rather to symbolise a sacred text or thought, and the figures, therefore, were not so much pictorially arranged, as composed with extreme monumental simplicity; thus, they not only partook of the general effect of the window, but the attention of the spectator, impressed with the solemn yet beautiful light, was, at the same time, filled with the holy thought conveyed by the subject, without being distracted by too great an individuality of parts.

The representation of shadow, strictly speaking, was not admissible, the composition consisting only of flat forms of the greatest simplicity. For this, even, there would seem to be just reasons: the light being transmitted through the glass to the spectator within, shadow would appear to be anomalous and out of place, since the illumination in such a case emanates from the figures themselves; moreover the simplicity of the shadowless forms was better suited to impress the eye from the distance at which such works must necessarily be viewed. Such would seem to be some of the principles which ought to regulate, and which in the best times did regulate, the design for painted glass.

An entirely different view of the art has however sprung up with its revival, and has obtained many advocates, especially on the Continent. It has been felt how greatly art has advanced in the hands of the historical painter since the times spoken of: that the principles of composition, of foreshortening, of perspective, of light and dark, and of the arrangement of colour, then quite unknown, have been discovered and developed; that drawing, then in its infancy and unaided by knowledge, has now arrived at maturity; and that science has given us power over the materials which they failed to possess, and enabled us to conquer difficulties which they considered insuperable; and it is asked why the painter on glass should not avail himself of all these advantages, to perfect his art and render it as pictorial as the works of his brethren. By artists who entertain these views, the surface of the window is treated almost as a canvas would be; the forms of the figures are large, even as the size of life; the draperies are massive, and the heads painted with great imitative skill and completeness. Chiaro-oscuro and perspective are studied, and foreshortening and pictorial attitudes in the figures supply the place of the monumental and statuesque delineations of the earlier artists; in fact everything is done to treat the window as a picture.

To the advocates of this style it may be objected, that a picture is specially intended to address itself to the mind and imagination only, while painted glass has a reference to use also: and that, apart from this consideration, each and every art has its own mode of rendering nature—not necessarily implying *deceptive* or complete imitation; thus, for instance, the art of the sculptor is a generalised imitation of form, and even the painter of high art does not desire to make his picture deceptively imitative, but listens with impatience to the remarks of the ignorant, who are apt to praise his work for this quality above others proper to it which they do not understand. An outline of Flaxman's fills the mind with a perfect sense of beauty and with the fulness of a poetical idea; surely, then, the flat and simple treatment of subjects in glass-painting, if such treatment is requisite for its utility and most in consonance with its other qualities, may be found sufficient to give as complete an expression to the pictorial rendering of a scripture truth as the material and situation of such works require.

The reader will readily recall examples of both these modes of treatment, and in the South Kensington collection are fine specimens of mediæval glass from the Sainte Chapelle at Paris, and of the more recent and more pictorial manner of the Munich school. The window by Professor Bertini, of Milan, is a beautiful example of the transparency treatment of glass. Here the forms are simple and broad, the masses of colour large, and the effect thoroughly that of a transparent picture, with all its details well drawn, carefully painted, and rounded by shadow; while the composition is arranged with regard to the masses of light and dark by colour. But instead of that general and harmonious effect of sobered light, which is so desirable in stained glass for the windows of a religious edifice, the effect is painful to the eye from its extreme brightness, and the window would irresistibly obtrude itself upon the attention of the spectator, and rather distract his thoughts than induce that solemn repose of mind which is so consistent with the place for which it is intended. It is to be observed also that the construction of the window is greatly in the way in these pictorial treatments, and that a false construction is too frequently adopted to the entire disregard of architectural fitness. The other method of treatment has many able exponents in this country, and the tendency of the modern school of glass-painters is, in many cases, to revert to the principles we have endeavoured to deduce from a study of the best works of mediæval artists.

It would seem to be a great fault in glass to have a prevailing tint or hue, since by a truly harmonious composition of colour such a result would be avoided. This is often the case with the modern French glass, as seen in some of the restored churches of Paris, more especially the pictorial glass, in which a warm, red hue is often present, sometimes to a painful extent : the flesh especially is hot, and dirty in the shadows. It is to be doubted, indeed, if, with all our knowledge of the harmony and complements of colours, we have yet attained to the principles by which the old glass-painters arranged their agreeable combinations. Whatever was the method, the effect was coolness of general tone : the flesh had little local colour, the prevailing tints of the draperies and accessories were blue, cool green, and amethyst, and even the red was cool, inclining to crimson. The brown hues of the flesh in the modern glass, together with its opacity, are often very disagreeable, and the effect of scarlet instead of crimson tends to increase the hot and glaring effect of the whole. In the Parisian churches, where ancient and modern glass is to be found side by side, even when the former is not of the best period, as in St. Germain l'Auxerrois, for instance, it is quite refreshing to turn the eye from the modern to the old glass, showing how far more harmonious the one is than the other.

In estimating the excellences of the one or the other methods of glass-painting we have spoken of, the superior durability of the earlier method is to be noticed; also the much smaller liability to accidents from the diminished size of the pane, and the comparatively small amount of damage done if a fracture does take place: an unlucky blow may immediately destroy the finest portion of a pictorial window, while it could do but small injury to a work on the older principle. These are minor merits, but to them may be added the greatly increased brilliancy of colour occasioned by the more frequent interposition of the dark line of the leading, and the lustre occasioned by the slight change of plane, in the smaller pieces of the early method bringing out thereby the richness of the glass, as the varied facets of the lapidary increase the lustre of the precious stone. Indeed it may be doubted if the subject of leading has had all the attention it so well deserves. The skilful manner in which this was executed in the early works is apparent from the preservation of the windows, unharmed by the storms and winds of centuries. It is certain that a varied surface was at times adopted in such works, for resisting, as has been supposed, the pressure of the winds: thus at Haddon Hall, in the long gallery, glazed in the reign of Elizabeth, each window is waved inwards and outwards over the whole surface, and each piece of glass cut to adapt it to this treatment: the result has been great durability, even although the lead itself is extremely narrow. These are, it is true, windows of uncoloured glass; but it may probably point to the use of some similar method in decorated windows, to enhance their brilliancy and increase their effect.

INLAID FLOORS, MOSAIC PAVEMENTS, INLAID TILES, ETC.

The ornament of this section of our manufactures seems to be in the soundest and most satisfactory state, the most free from false principles, the most thoroughly amenable to true ones.

Although this no doubt partly arises from the conditions of the manufacture, it is, in a degree, to be attributed to other causes. The modern introduction of such works in England was at a fortunate time, when the attention of the ecclesiologists and of able artists was called to the revival of mediæval art, and to the study of the best works of Greece and Italy. The designer, therefore, started upon just principles, and continues to adhere to them, even repudiating some of what must be considered errors in the ancient works which have been handed down to us, such as those arrangements of light and dark inlays, giving the appearance of relief, which are found occasionally even in the best ancient examples.

FIG. 4.

We here reproduce a few specimens of floor and wall tiles, which appear to us to combine a true application of principle with a thorough comprehension of the necessities of the material.

The illustration (Fig. 4) is of an enamelled wall-tile, imitated from one found at Salisbury, and is given here to show the mode in which flowers were used as ornaments in such works by the mediæval artists. The flower is displayed perfectly flat, in one colour, and arranged geometrically.

Fig. 5 is given as a more intricate treatment on the same sound principles, and is from a design by Mr. Pugin.

Fig. 6 is an impressed and enamelled tile of a Moorish pattern, for covering the surface of a wall with an ornamental texture, and with a broken harmonious richness of colour, in very durable materials, for which purpose it is admirably adapted. Many novel and praiseworthy works in burnt and coloured clay are now produced to facilitate the application of design and colour to the exterior of buildings. Among others, a species of Majolica ware, with ornament in relief, coloured with delicate tints, intended to be introduced into friezes, string-courses, panels, &c., and other combinations of the art of the designer with the skill of the tile-maker and the potter, which will enable the architect to break the monotonous surface of brick buildings, and introduce ornamental forms and colour without the necessity of resorting to plaster and

FIG. 5.

stucco, so long the wretched resource for such purposes. From the geological position of London, bricks must always be the prevailing material for building purposes : such means, therefore, for the safe introduction of colour and ornament, are especially desirable, and should be carefully studied, that the most judicious and sound principles of ornamentation may be adopted in these newly-revived materials. It is curious to see how instantly the removal of the excise-duty on bricks was followed by the infusion of a new life into the manufacture, both as to novel forms and the application of coloured ornament to their surface; it must be remarked, however, that the ornament of each separate brick should be perfect in itself as well as perfect in combinations.

From the general use of carpets, considered, as they are, as a necessary comfort in this country, inlaid floors are far less used here than on the Continent, and we therefore obtain our chief supply of marqueterie work for floors from abroad. The principle of ornamentation, of course, is the same as that for mosaics and other inlays; care, however, should be taken to select wood without a strongly marked form in its grain, since this is likely to interfere with the pattern of the inlay in general; also right-lined figures are preferable to curved ones, in consequence of there being less need of crossing the grain of the wood in cutting.

FIG. 6.

PAPER AND OTHER HANGINGS.

If the use of such materials is borne in mind, the proper decoration for them will at once be evident, since materials of this class ought to bear the same relation to the objects in the room that a background does to a picture. In art, a background, if well designed, has its own distinctive features, yet these are to be so far suppressed and subdued as not to invite especial attention; while as a whole it ought to be entirely subservient to supporting and enhancing the principal figures—the subject of the picture. The decoration of a wall, if designed on good principles, has a like office: it is a background to the furniture, the objects of art, and the occupants of the apartment. It may enrich the general effect, and add to magnificence, or be made to lighten or deepen the character of the chamber: it may appear to temper the heat of summer, or to give a sense of warmth and comfort to the winter: it may have the effect of increasing the size of a saloon, or of closing-in the walls of a library or study: all which, by a due adaptation of colour, can be easily accomplished. But, like the background to which it has been compared, although its ornament may have a distinctive character for any of these purposes, it must be subdued, and uncontrasted in light and shade; strictly speaking, it should be flat and conventionalized, and lines or forms which are harsh or cutting on the ground should be as far as possible avoided, except where necessary to give expression to the ornamentation. Imitative treatments are objectionable on principle, both as intruding on the sense of flatness, and as being too *attractive* in their details and colours to be sufficiently retiring and unobtrusive. Some of the best examples of correct style as well in paper as in silk, velvet, and other hangings, are manufactured in varied treatments of *texture* in a self-colour; as for instance of flock on plain or satined ground in paper, of tabby and satin in silk hangings, of stamped forms or cutting in velvet, or the same contrast of pattern with the ground in various mixed stuffs. By these means the ornament is necessarily flat, and does not disturb the general effect. With the slightest attention to the choice of form such a design can hardly be in bad taste, whilst great elegance and beauty often arises from such treatments. Next to these, graduated tints of the same colour produce a safe and quiet ornamentation for such fabrics; or gold upon a coloured ground, where the gold is sparingly distributed and the colour not too strongly contrasted; since in all cases a general *tone* of surface is to be sought for rather than pronounced individual forms. Further richness may be obtained by the judicious use of two or more colours, arranged either according to the ancient method of harmony, that is separated from each other by bands of black, white, or gold, or contrasted and enhanced by their complementaries, and enriched by flock in either case; in the latter case gold may be used with advantage. But we ever find that the combination of many colours, though it may increase expense from the number of blocks, is far from producing richness in a like degree, while it has often quite the contrary effect, and results only in poverty and meanness.

It is necessary, however, to advert to a perfectly different treatment of these materials quite at variance with these rules, and bound by no such principles, by which paper-hanging becomes a pseudo-decoration, the wall being divided into compartments often irrespective of architectural construction, with pilasters, friezes, and mouldings imitated in false relief on its surface, and having compositions of pictures, statues, hangings, flowers, fruits, &c., skilfully designed and well drawn, and, it may be, often most ably blocked for the purpose of printing. This is, however, at best but a sham decoration amenable to no laws, necessarily false in light and shade, often constructively inapplicable, and always impertinent and obtrusive, and should be left to those who, while desirous of display, are too much wanting in taste to be annoyed at its untruth and extravagance. Such a mode of decoration may perhaps be not quite out of place in the saloon of a theatre, in cafés, or in taverns, but it ought to be confined to such localities, and should only be used there until the general taste is so far instructed that the public will no longer tolerate gaudy shams and false magnificence.

The same laws which ought to govern design for paper-hangings would, therefore, appear proper to regulate hangings of other fabrics, tapestries, &c. Although far from regarding ornament in that exclusive spirit which would reject what is beautiful when it does not agree with the requisitions of a theory, it must be obvious that pictorial and picturesque treatments for such fabrics are wrong whenever they intrude on the domain of another art. Thus, figures, landscapes, fruits, and flowers, when rendered as they would be in works of fine art, are almost of necessity inferior to the pictures they imitate, even when they are as skilfully and wonderfully wrought as in the works produced by the national establishment of the Gobelins, where every effort of skill and science has been most successfully used for their manufacture and embellishment. Indeed, it is a matter of doubt whether custom, and the authority of great names and of past times, are not the causes of the continued admiration of such decorations, which perhaps we rather persuade ourselves we like than are fully satisfied with.

Our modern designs for hangings are too often florid and gaudy compositions, consisting of architectural ornament in relief, with imitative flowers and foliage. In some of the cleverest of them the flowers and foliage are perspectively rendered with the full force of their natural colours, and light and shade; moreover, they are often three or four times as large as nature, whereby the size of a room would be apparently diminished. This florid style is mainly prevalent among French manufacturers, and from the extent to which this country is supplied with wall-papers and tapestries from France, these errors of style are liable to be imported into England with all the added influence of French taste.

In all these florid and pictorial treatments of surface as contrasted with the correct treatment for wall-papers, there is evidently no distinction in the minds of the designers between the principles applicable or permissible in the one class of works, and those ornamental principles which alone should govern the other. Thus pictorial imitation is the rule throughout; not only pictorial renderings of flowers as ornament, but occasionally imitations of silk hangings with their plaited folds, of lace and muslin, of fringes, of stone and metal mouldings in high relief; but also (even in high-priced papers) imitations of landscapes, birds, trees, and architecture, which would thus be multiplied interminably over the walls. Thus, notwithstanding the superior taste in the management of tints and the discrimination of colours, which is the result of the causes before alluded to, or of the better education of the French workmen, it is difficult to find abroad a paper in really good taste.

Having laid down certain principles upon which this class of manufactures and fabrics should be designed with a view to the true use of materials, and to the avoidance of unnecessary display, by the proper application of ornament, it is impossible to refrain from speaking in high terms of the influence upon our modern manufactures of the elder Pugin. Some may object to the exclusiveness of the style of his designs, and to its too purely ecclesiastical and traditional character, even in domestic works; but for just principles of decoration, for beautiful details, and for correct use of materials, we cannot too highly praise the works he inspired. Thus, in his paper-hangings, for instance, there is no throwing away of many blocks to obtain richness, when one or two can be made sufficient: there is a perfect flatness and a subdued harmony of colour in all such works; and if Tudor roses and heraldic lions are sometimes too pronounced, and there is occasionally a little excess of ornament, richness is generally obtained at the smallest sacrifice of means, and without any sacrifice of truth. It is difficult to over-estimate the important effect for good brought about mainly by the writings and designs of Pugin, and to omit the mention of his name in any work on modern design would be a grievous oversight.

The lately-introduced processes of printing paper-hangings by such machinery as is used for cotton goods, and of applying many colours from one block, are, we fear, likely to create a style of ornamentation for such fabrics of the most depraved kind. The largeness and flatness of details attainable by block-printing are less suited to cylinder-printing than more minute details, and the new processes offer ready means of applying several colours at a small expense—the reverse of what has hitherto been the case; hence the effort has been to impress as many tints as possible on paper, and excellence is reckoned rather by the number of colours than by any other quality. Thus we are informed that works are printed in "sixteen colours," in "fourteen colours," &c., the works themselves evidencing the absence of all knowledge of the effective arrangement of colour; while violent, crude, and harsh tints are too often used to give greater impression of this *excellence!* and the result is littleness and extreme meanness; in fact, such papers are, in point of design, much inferior to those printed in two colours by the same machinery. Well-considered design, thoroughly adapted for this process, would enable the manufacturer to unite good taste with extreme cheapness; whereas the only present result is, by increased labour, to detract from the beauty of the ornamentation.

EXTERIOR AND OTHER METAL WORK.

The works, in metal, of this section with which we are mainly concerned consist of fountains, and ornamental iron-work in gates and balconies, and of castings for door-panels and lamp-pillars. The best of the metal fountains come so nearly within the limits of fine art, that their consideration is almost beyond our scope while dealing with simple decoration. Notwithstanding all that has been said about the incongruity of our climate with public fountains, there are undoubtedly long periods of the year, and those when London is most crowded as well with her own resident population as with visitors, when such works are not only extremely ornamental, but when an exhausting atmosphere would render them really useful and refreshing. The motion of water, at any season, has a great charm, and is peculiar in its power of giving pleasure even in the simplest jet or fall, agreeably and artistically disposed; and ornamental arrangements for its full display would not only be picturesque additions to our city, which offers so many localities for their adoption, but would afford to our artists motives for combinations of figures with ornamental decoration. A means might thus, perhaps, be afforded of once more uniting fine and ornamental art, which, sadly to the deterioration of public taste, have for so long a time been almost wholly separated. It may be doubted if the public would willingly part with even the tame and commonplace repetitions which adorn Trafalgar Square; and those who have had the pleasure of enjoying the fountains of Italy and France will be quite prepared to judge of the effect which more skilfully-designed structures would have on the public mind here.

Such works as gates, balconies, and panels, when made in iron, are for the greater part, in cast-metal, which of late years, from its capability of receiving cheap ornamentation, has almost wholly superseded wrought iron for these purposes. Where the object is intended to be fixed and immovable, as a balcony or panel, cast work is not unsuitable, and is capable of much beauty of ornamental design. In these the ornament should add to the strength by its numerous articulations, yet be light and elegant in its forms. Works of this kind, too, are generally of a size to admit of being cast in one piece, ensuring thereby strength and lightness by continuity of parts. But in cast-iron constructions intended to be movable, as in the various kinds of gates, a very different character of design is necessary; partly because entire casting is not always possible, both from the difficulty of running the metal into the numerous ramifications of the ornament in works of such increased size, and partly from the fear of warping in the cooling. The great expense of a mould is also saved by forming the ornament of a series of parts. This leads to the necessity of framing the work in wrought, and applying the ornamental details in cast-iron; but hence results this evil, that the ornament has little constructive use, and is apt to look rather an addition than an integral part of the work. Moreover, cast-iron ornament is necessarily far heavier than that composed of wrought iron, owing to the extreme brittleness of the cast-metal: this heaviness is sadly opposed to its real constructive strength in the manner usually adopted for putting together. The ornamental parts of such structures being pinned or screwed into the framing, there are smaller points of attachment than in wrought iron ; the parts bed themselves less perfectly at the junction, since it is impossible to assist this union with the hammer, and the metal has small tenacity, and easily breaks with any sudden jar. There is thus much less power to support, while there is of necessity much greater weight to bear; and without very careful and well-considered design, making the ornament as far as possible a brace to the work, the whole is apt to be an insecure aggregation of parts, without constructive unity or truth. In large objects, cast in one piece, such difficulties are readily surmounted, as weight can then be made to add strength, instead of detracting from it. In the old hammer-wrought gates, the ornament was not only a truly integral part of the work, but most materially assisted in the general support. Thus great lightness and elegance were, in this case, consistent with great strength, since the ornamental details supplied a means, not only of tying and bracing the work together, but also of preventing the front of the gate from drooping with its own weight, to the great hindrance of its use, and which defect in modern cast works of this kind has often to be overcome by the use of friction-rollers—a make-shift that the older workmen would have despised. When, therefore, we consider the varied beauty of which wrought iron is capable, its far greater durability, its tenacity and power of resisting accidents, the individuality of design which arises from its being wrought by the hand instead of cast in a mould (thereby leaving the fancy and the feeling of the workman untrammelled), it is satisfactory to find that a return to wrought iron for such uses is beginning to be evident.

We frequently come across garden-seats and chairs in cast-metal, which are principally to be noticed from the great want of due consideration of the material evidenced in their design : thus sometimes they are ornamentally constructed of branches and foliage naturally imitated, or of branches alone ; while, in others, carved and flowing lines are given to the back, arms, and legs of the seat, adding nothing to the comfort of their use, and sadly detracting from the form properly belonging to such works. It must be confessed, indeed, that the tendency to consider the ornament before either the requirements of the material, or the use to which the work is to be applied, is but too evident in many of the works in metal in this class. The uses of iron for constructive purposes have ever been increasing since the Exhibition of 1851 pointed the way to a fit method of introducing this material. In America, in some of the principal cities, iron is made to do the work of almost every other building material, and often, where it is made to take the place of and to assume the characteristics of brick and stone, with the most unfortunate results. We learn that a Trans-Atlantic founder thinks nothing of turning out an entire house front in cast-iron to order.

CHAPTER IX.

ON DOMESTIC AND OTHER FURNITURE.

FURNITURE and upholstery constitute, perhaps, the bulk of the manufactures which must receive our attention, and we shall find that many of the principles laid down in our first section will have a direct bearing upon works of this class.

In endeavouring to state principles which may serve as general rules for the furniture designer, it will without difficulty be conceded that, having some specific purpose in view, his first consideration should be *perfect adaptation to intended use*; this may appear so obvious a truism as to want no enforcement, but a visit to a modern drawing-room will speedily undeceive us, for there we see a multitude of objects offending against this rule : in some of them use is almost entirely overlooked, or has been evidently quite a secondary consideration, whilst in others it partially gives way either to effect or ornament. Thus we find a table of costly manufacture which has ornament in solid relief on its upper surface, and a fire-grate which evidently requires a glass case, since fire and smoke must be the worst enemies to such a polished marvel. We see, again, a pianoforte, surrounded by bristling bulrushes, which must always be catching in the dresses of those who approach it, and with hardly a right line in any part of it; and chairs so heavy that they must be fixtures instead of movables; while of minor incongruities, the instances are too numerous to specify. Manufacturers should aim at obtaining the greatest amount of convenience and accommodation in the least space, in order that the furniture may be as suitable as possible to the size and uses of the apartment in which it is placed.

Another consideration to be attended to is stability of construction, *apparent* as well as *real*; the first being necessary to satisfy the eye, the last being indispensable to excellence and durability. Thus, as we have seen, the legs of articles of furniture, designed in the style of Louis XV., are often broken in the centre across the grain of the wood, or have their base of support far within the perpendicular line of the bearing; a fault which, though it does not actually render them unstable, yet offends the eye as much as if they were really insecure.

The constructive forms, moreover, should not be obscured by the ornament, but rather brought out by it; nor should all portions be equally decorated, but only such parts as friezes, pilasters, capitals, pillars, or panels; herein simplicity is the safest guide to beauty. Over-enrichment, indeed, destroys itself, and it would not be difficult to point out works of the greatest pretension and the most costly workmanship, which are completely spoilt by this fault. Cabinets entirely covered with carving, the very stiles and rails being as decorated as the panels and pilasters: metal chandeliers, with leaves and flowers in as great profusion as in nature: papier-mâché hidden under a surface of pearl and gold. It should be remembered that contrast is one of the first elements of pleasure, and that *repose* is one of the most valued excellencies of art; thus simplicity serves as the background to ornament, as the setting to the gem, or the foil that enhances the beauty of the jewel; and the good artist is as much shown in the economy of his labour as the bad one is by over-enrichment.

In following out our principle that ornament should arise out of construction, the work, abstractedly, should be constructed and then decorated; not that it is meant that the ornament should be *applied* to the object, but (as in wood for instance) carved from it; thus the leg formed for support, the pilaster or column for bearing, may be lightened and enriched by cutting away from the block or slab, not by adding to it. In his natural state man is a true workman in this respect, and works on just principles without knowing it. The New Zealander or South-Sea Islander first *forms* his war-club or his paddle of the shape best adapted for use, and then carves the surface to ornament it. The Swiss peasant, or the shepherd of our own hills, works in a similar way. Such also is the case in the works of Eastern nations, as is particularly exemplified in their choice sandal-wood carvings. Here the natural and the refined taste agree, for the best ornamental wood-carving of the Renaissance is on this principle, low in relief, seldom projecting beyond the surface of the pilaster, or the framing of the panel.

In wood-carving care should be taken not only to have the relief so managed as to guard the work as much as possible from accidental injury, but the designer should seek to adapt the forms of the ornament to the direction of the grain when it is open or free, and the work should be framed with a view to this consideration; moreover, ornamental carving should not be applied to wood of strongly-marked party-coloured grain, but that which is homogeneous in colour should be selected for the purpose, in order that the ornamental forms may as little as possible be interfered with by being mixed up with the lines and colours of the grain. It is curious how much costly and skilful labour has been thrown away from inattention to such minor considerations as these.

CABINET-WORK AND FURNITURE OF ALL KINDS.

The furniture of a man's house should indeed be well designed, well constructed, and judiciously ornamented, for, as it is constantly under his hand and eye, defects overlooked at first, or disregarded for some showy excellence, grow into great grievances, when, after they have become an offence, the annoyance daily increases. Here at least utility should be the first object, and, as simplicity rarely offends, that ornament which is the most simple in style will be likely to give the most lasting satisfaction. Yet how seldom is this consideration duly attended to! The ornament too often consists largely of *imitative* carving; bunches of fruit, flowers, game, and utensils of various kinds in swags and festoons of the most massive size and the boldest impost, attached indiscriminately and without meaning to bedsteads, sideboards, bookcases, pier-glasses, &c., rarely carved from the members of the work itself, but merely applied as so much putty-work or papier-mâché might be. The laws of ornament are as completely set at defiance as those of use and convenience. Many of these works, instead of being useful, would require a rail to keep off the household. We see a sideboard, for instance, with garlands of imitative flowers projecting so far from the slab as to require a "long arm" to reach across them, and ever liable to be chipped and broken; and cabinets and bookcases so bristling with walnut-wood flowers and oaken leaves, as to put use out of the question. Now, such treatments, while they are not only not ornamental, are also not beautiful, and only enter into competition with stamped leather and gutta-percha. There is great reason to doubt if this merely imitative carving is ever just in principle, when applied ornamentally to furniture; for, although the masterly chisel of Grinling Gibbons has raised it to great favour in this country, and although it may be tolerated when executed skilfully, yet it becomes absolutely unbearable under less skilful hands, and when it is lavished in such profusion as we used to find it. Happily this state of things is dying out under improved culture. In France there is far less of this false mode of decoration, and a better sense of ornament prevails; the works being more frequently designed in the traditional styles. A modification of the Renaissance is principally used, and in this the ornament is in low relief, and does not interfere with use; although false construction is a vice of that period, which has not been remedied in their modern works, but is sometimes even exaggerated.

The style of Louis XV. lingers in France; its playfulness of line and surface, its varied treatment and mixture of materials, together with its showiness, still command favour with the multitude. The surfaces of works in this style are curved, when practicable; they are veneered in party-coloured woods, and panels are formed by or-molu mouldings, often in both instances completely at variance with the true construction; and occasionally the panels are filled with porcelain enamels, the whole having at least a gay and sparkling appearance. In English adaptations of the style, instead of the treatment above described, the bold scrolls and shell-forms used in the decoration of rooms at that period are carved in all their coarseness on furniture. Such works bear out the remark before made, that these forms were especially adapted for gilding, and, indeed, are hardly bearable except when so treated, or when made of metal. This becomes even more apparent when full-coloured woods are used, such as mahogany; in this material the ornament is even more coarse and heavy than in lighter-coloured wood. Since, however, the vendors of cheap furniture have adopted this manner as a cheap and flashy decoration for their goods, it is to be hoped that it will soon be entirely proscribed, or retained only by such dealers.

Those designers who unreservedly adopt the ornament of past times must, of course, apply it to their works without any peculiar significance or connected idea, but merely for its beautiful forms, elegance, grace, or richness. Where, however, any significant allusion, sentiment, or happy idea can be embodied in the ornament, uniting it with the use and intent of the work on which it is to be placed, it will have a charm which is otherwise wanting. Not that this want is peculiar to the application of traditional ornament, since the designer in the natural or imitative manner seldom attempts any connexion between his decoration and the work to which it is to be applied. There seems no fitness, for instance, in surrounding the frame of a pier-glass with dead birds, game, shell-fish, nets, &c., although they may be excellent specimens of carving; nor is it clear why eagles should support a sideboard, or dogs form the arms of an elbow-chair; nor, again, why swans should make their nests under a table, at the risk of having their necks broken by every one seated at it. Indeed, in most cases, as such imitative forms cannot in the strict sense be called ornament, they almost challenge inquiry as to why they have been adopted, and only disappoint us when we find that their application has been without motive: this is not the case with traditional ornament, which, like the current coin, is accepted at once without inquiry.

When we turn from such imitative works to furniture designed strictly in accordance with the rules of a traditional style, we feel that there is often a cold propriety about it which requires consideration before we can admire it. There is a strong movement at the present time in favour of a so-called mediæval treatment. It may perhaps be objected that the general forms of furniture in this style want variety, and this is rendered more apparent by the florid lines of works of the ordinary type; but the principal reason will be found to arise from a due consideration of the true constructive treatment of *wood*, which is ill adapted to curved forms on account of its grain, and requires horizontal and perpendicular lines as the basis of framing. Some credit is due to this revival of a better and purer state of things, to the return to the old paths, and to the avoidance of the present mere sensualism of ornament. Yet it is not on this account, but as examples of careful and strict adhesion to true *principles* of construction and ornamentation, that the works in this style deserve commendation.

Some of the greatest faults in our furniture are unsuitableness to uses and false construction: it will often be found to be as skilful in execution as it is deficient in adaptation to its intended purposes. In cabinets large spaces are thrown away, and therefore, though occupying much room, there is little that is available for use; the centre space, with its canopy (though pretty), has no apparent purpose, and it is quite disproportioned to the size of the wings, while it is also deficient in the appearance of support. The bookcases have often the same fault of room thrown away and of unsuitableness to use, besides displaying a false adaptation of Gothic stone forms to wood-carving. This latter fault is elsewhere also largely prevalent; it will be found to be a common error in foreign furniture. Thus we have a wardrobe which would be more characteristic as an oratory, and a bookcase with arches that support nothing, and buttresses which have no thrusts to resist. Indeed it should be remembered that the *arch* is not a wooden, but essentially a stone construction; it will be evident, on a moment's consideration, that it is a means of obtaining support by a number of separate small parts, the reverse of timber construction. It ought, therefore, to be well considered before being used in wood, wherein it should arise rather from coupled knees or brackets introduced to strengthen horizontal beams, than as an independent form.

Sham construction is another error to which we have already alluded, not only of the kind before spoken of,—the suppression of the true constructive forms, as panels, framing, &c., and the giving of undue prominence to others,—but also that where those portions which are intended for support (as, for instance, columns in cabinets, legs in sideboards, &c.) are made to move from under the parts intended to be supported when opening the doors of the furniture. This is a common case in cabinets designed in the Renaissance style, and has the authority of some of the best early specimens; nevertheless, it is a constructive fault, and is instanced because it is the source of many like errors of a more glaring kind, as where legs are made to remove, or where the whole front of a cabinet or wardrobe is made into doors hanging to the sides without a framed facia and hanging style, and where both the side and centre columns (when such are so used as decorations) are made to move with the doors.

The great defect in all our more ambitious furniture is the want of art-power in the workman. In this respect we are still sadly behind continental nations. Whenever the human figure is used as ornament in English works it is pretty sure to be faulty. The figure may be well composed, may be evidently designed in good taste, since that is often the work of a superior artist; but in the execution it is almost always misunderstood and spoiled. The extremities are finished without knowledge of the internal structure, the fingers, toes, and joints have no bones within the skin, but that "gummy" undecided treatment which evidences the ignorance of the workman. In wood-carving this is equally apparent, even when it consists only of ornamental forms. Very often in such work the "design" of the ornament would seem to be by the same unskilled hand that carved it, since it is mostly out of place, coarse, and merely "natural" in style, and rarely reaches beyond the expression of the most commonplace thought, or the imitation of the commonest fruits and flowers. Success in rendering either the human figure or animals, when in life and motion, can only be the result of knowledge attained by a careful study of the structure of the bony frame-work and of the moving muscles; and thus it is the want of such anatomical knowledge and of a proper training in art that causes the deficiency we are obliged to notice in our furniture, and which compels the carver to confine himself to mere works of imitation, knowing that higher flights are beyond his powers. This deficiency of power and skill in the human figure is only an additional evidence of the want of better education for our art-workmen. They need to have proper treatises prepared for them, laying down the principles of ornament, and giving them a thorough foundation in practical geometry, form, proportion, and, above all, in anatomy, together with a careful education of the hand and eye. Unless the manufacturers of this country are soon awakened to our deficiencies, and prepared to make great sacrifices to support the government art schools, and to enable and induce their workmen to study in them, we must be content to lag still further behind as the world advances, and for the future to be manufacturers of cheap goods, leaving excellence and beauty to our continental neighbours.

HARDWARE.

Under this head are comprised grates, fenders, fire-irons, stoves, gas-fittings, lamps, and various miscellaneous applications; the whole being largely connected with ornamental design. The works in this section, however, are not more miscellaneous in their use than they are in their style of ornamentation: thus we see in our shops Greek candelabra adapted to many uses, Gothic chandeliers and Renaissance lamps, with a pretty large sprinkling of the forms and ornament of Louis XIV. and XV., to which is to be added the *natural style* before alluded to, which, adopting foliage or flowers as its leading idea, presents them as they grow, without any constructive or architectural arrangement whatever. Yet even this is encouraging, since it indicates a desire for something more than mere reproductions of the antique, or that *mêlée* of ornament which the ignorant gather from many works, and re-assemble without taste or appropriateness. In a great portion of the works in metal French taste is found largely to prevail; nor is this to be wondered at, since, for a long time, the lively fancy and invention of many excellent French artists have been directed to designing and modelling for these goods; ably seconded, also, by trained and educated workmen capable of appreciating their labours, and completing them by skilful casting, chasing, and fitting. But the tendency of the French mind towards display has resulted in over-ornamentation, and it is unfortunate that this fault is rather a merit in the eyes of the world, and has been eagerly adopted by the manufacturers of other nations, more especially by our own; that which is meretricious being retained, whilst what is really excellent in French design, and especially in French workmanship, is overlooked by them, or is found unattainable.

Moreover, whilst the most able French artists in metal, eschewing the gaudy style of Louis XV., have returned to a modified form of the Renaissance, and have given it somewhat of newness of character, the English designers for hardware too often still adhere either to the contorted style first named, or they produce works composed of ornaments pirated from all times and all nations, put together without any sense of construction, without selection and without fitness. Such works are a thorough chance-medley, disgraceful to our manufacturers, and

FIG. 7.

they make us look back to the simpler forms of the Middle-ages with respect and regret.

Let anyone examine the characteristic simplicity of the candlestick here engraved (Fig. 7), made from a design by Mr. W. Pugin, adapted as it is for use, standing firmly, capable of being handled, light yet strong, and compare it with the showy works of this class we commonly see, so *ragged* and tangled with ornament that all characteristic form is lost, branched arms, bristling with foliage which weighs down rather than braces and supports them, with perhaps a bunch of flimsy chains dangling in the way of those who would touch or lift them, or two or three Parian Cupids basking at the foot, or bearing up the candles; and having, where the hand should grasp the stem to lift the candelabrum, the ornament so sharp and thorny that to touch it would be impossible. In making such a comparison can we do otherwise than feel that the one is honest, useful, characteristic, and therefore beautiful, whilst the others are flashy and grotesque, full of little prettinesses, which some misname "ideas," put together without any leading motive, and having no definite character or true construction?

The faults of English design for hardware are obvious to every one; the error of the French designers is equally open to the most superficial observer. In the great mass of their works there is no rest for the eye—the whole surface is nothing but ornament. Thus, for instance, the French art-bronzes have justly obtained a wide reputation, and the works of Denière, Pradier, Méne, and other French artists, are sought for all over Europe; but when such become a part of manufacture, and liable to be classed as hardware, art is overlaid with ornament, and the skill of the workman is directed to that which degrades the work, and sadly militates against good taste. Thus, figures designed with much fancy, and modelled with ability and vigour, are vulgarised from the imitation of fur and of the texture of the garments, of buckles, buttons, and ties of the dress, of chain or plate armour or weapons, whilst the homogeneity of the bronze is no longer retained, but various parts of dress are treated in various tints of the metal; and all the different qualities of surface, such as tooling, frosting, and burnishing, in which it is but just to say the workmen are most skilful, are brought into play to *enrich* the effect; while sometimes we have, in addition, combinations of many materials, such as marble, porcelain, ivory, and bronze, united in a single work.

Another class of works are those anomalous candelabra composed of porcelain vases filled with a bunch of flowers in or-molu, a few bearing candles amongst a number of barren branches, the whole being a bush of glitter and burnish. This is the direction which naturalism in ornament takes in France. Such works have a total absence of constructive feeling, and an equal want of proper treatment of metal; to add to their finery, an épergne of artificial flowers is often mixed up with metallic ones, as a centre-piece for the dinner-table. The error, however, does not wholly rest with the designer, since it will be long before he has a public sufficiently educated to relish the amount of plainness which is absolutely necessary to give the true value to each part enriched.

Grates rank among the principal works in hardware to which ornamental design is applied, and it is gratifying also to find that the design and decoration of these goods has greatly improved in the last few years. There is, however, an evident tendency to do too much, and it is incumbent on designers for such goods carefully to avoid this, and to endeavour to restrain manufacturers from such treatments of the metals as lead to gaudiness and glare, and by which, at the same time, the grate itself is rendered less useful. The great secret, after constructive use has been considered, consists in the proper and judicious treatment of the materials, which offer great advantages for contrast, either with or without the introduction of bronze or or-molu. True excellence will be found here also to be closely allied with simplicity, a moderate use of ornament and of the burnisher, and the contrast of broad flat masses of plain metal with ornamented or burnished mouldings, with inlays of brass, or with bronze and or-molu ornaments. The arched form which has generally been adopted for grate-fronts is architecturally suitable as supporting the chimney breast, and agreeable in outline, giving ample opportunity for ornament in the mouldings of the arch, as well as in the spandrels, besides having sufficient surface of metal to serve as a contrast to the ornament; moreover, it is not likely to interfere with the architectural arrangement of the mantel-piece to which it may have to be fitted. Several grates designed by the late Mr. A. Stevens, decorative in character, and of great general merit, will be found in the Museum. The one engraved (Fig. 8) is constructively simple, and sufficiently ornamented for its office as an article of furniture, while it displays most judicious use of materials. The face is of ground, cast metal, the ornamented moulding of pale bronze, with the leafage of brass, and the figure

FIG. 8.

bronzed, while some semi-burnished lines about the fire give a very chaste and tasteful effect; the fender is also of bronze and brass, with the leading lines burnished. Much more ornament than this would raise the grate out of its right place in the scale of furniture, and draw undue attention to it; its sober simplicity is more to be commended than many more highly ornamented. It can never be too much insisted on, that ornament loses its value when it overloads a work, and that large unornamented spaces are required to enhance and give zest to the decorated parts. As we descend to grates designed by inferior artists, we find excess substituted for excellence, and works of such brilliant gaudiness of surface as to be quite unfitted for their intended use; indeed, the process of keeping them in order would seem to require that a whitesmith should form part of our establishment, or that the housemaid should have a practical education to enable her to take to pieces the elaborate constructions which would come under her care, independently of the skill required to clean them.

It is tiresome to repeat what has so often before been said, that use ought to be considered before ornament; yet no section of furniture suffers more from neglect of this rule than that comprised under hardware. In some cases this shows itself in applying a form or construction suited for one use, to another for which it is quite inapplicable. Thus we find some French chandeliers, which at first sight seem cleverly designed and show a skilful treatment of the metal, but which, on examination, are seen to consist of a large central lamp, which alone is intended to give light, surrounded by a circle of branches bearing sham candles, not intended or prepared in any way for illumination, but introduced merely to allow of a little extra ornament. From the same cause results the impertinent *application* of figures, in bronze or in Parian; a fertile source of bad taste. These are too often merely added to the work, and not constructively treated, and thus seem to have no real relation to the forms they are connected with. Hence the manufacturer is enabled to adapt the same figure to many purposes, and to the most opposite uses; sometimes at the base of a chandelier, sometimes at the top, and sometimes perched upon the branches. Profitable to the manufacturer this may be, but it is as completely opposed to every just principle of design as to every hope of progress or good taste.

In the treatment of metal the rendering of the surface demands the most careful study, since much of the beauty of a work results from this being properly understood. No doubt the true lustre of metal is only given in the burnished state; but when burnishing is introduced in any quantity it becomes not only tormenting to the eye but wants contrast to bring out its brilliancy. Moreover, by its glitter it obscures ornamental forms, which rarely look sharp or clear in their details under this treatment. When figures or animals, introduced for decoration, are burnished, their true form is almost undistinguishable on account of this glitter and the reflection from the polished surface, and this together with the pressure of the tool completely destroys all details of forms and surface. Yet we find that many important works have the figures entirely burnished. The evil caused by a glittering surface in such works is duly appreciated by the French artists, who have wisely adopted bronze as the material for figures in the baser metals, and have overcome the difficulty by oxidation in their works in silver. A medium state of the surface between mat and burnished, though much to be desired, is not always obtainable, nor has it perhaps been sufficiently sought. Bronze, however, from its colour, partially supplies this want; and the mixed metals, and ground cast-iron from its duller polish, afford good contrasts to burnished iron or steel.

While our use of burnish often tends to blur and destroy form, the older workmen took advantage of a polished surface to produce ornament; this may be seen in some of the old church chandeliers, of which the central trunk, consisting of a plain turned shaft, seems richly reeded when the branches are lighted, merely by the reflection of the lights on the metal.

In most of the modern works, burnished and matted surfaces seem to be used indifferently or at random, instead of applying the burnisher to give variety to recurring forms, or to enhance leading lines. These are often entirely matted or tooled, and those parts burnished which will give the greatest flutter and glitter to the object.

The facilities which modern mechanism gives to the production of ornament, and consequently to over-ornamentation, have already been adverted to. It is to be hoped that in view of these facilities manufacturers will see their own interest, and seek the best designs at any cost, since these will frequently be found to combine cheapness of production and simplicity with good taste.

CARPETS.

The use of these fabrics suggests the true principle of design for their ornamentation; which is governed by the laws before given for flat surfaces, where the object is rather to treat the whole as a background than to call particular attention to the ornamentation. Flatness should be one of the principles in decorating a surface continually under the feet; therefore all architectural relief ornaments, and all *imitations* of fruit, shells, and other solid or hard substances, or even of flowers, strictly speaking, are the more improper the more imitatively they are rendered. As a field or ground for other objects, the attention should hardly be called to carpets by strongly-marked forms or compartments, or by violent contrasts of light and dark, or colour; but graduated shades of the same colour, or a distribution of colours nearly equal in scale of light and dark, should be adopted; secondaries and tertiaries, or neutralised primaries being used rather than pure tints, and lights introduced merely to give expression to the forms. Under such regulations as to flatness and contrast, either geometrical forms, or scrolls clothed with foliation in any style, leaves, flowers, or other ornament, may be used, which, with borders and compartment arrangements, and the use of diaper treatments, leave ample room for variety and for the inventive skill of the artist. It may be thought impossible or unnecessary to confine the designer too strictly by such laws, and they are, indeed, rather stated from a sense of their truth than with an immediate hope of their thorough acceptance, but at any rate they may serve as curbs to extravagance of design, and as guide-marks to lead back the errant designer to the paths of consistency. In speaking of designs for carpets we turn first to France, because the importance of her national manufacture of these fabrics must claim our first consideration. The establishments under royal or national aid have carried these fabrics to the highest pitch of excellence in all that relates to skill of manufacture, brilliancy of colour, and magnificence of design. In the face of the many and rare excellences exhibited by them, both of handicraft and scientific knowledge, the chemist and the botanist having united their sciences with the invention and taste of the painter, it may seem daring to reprobate the ornamentation of such costly works; but their very excellence has so largely contributed to the spread of bad taste and false principles in such fabrics, that it becomes a positive duty, in the face even of the highest authorities, to object to the principles on which they are ornamented, if we would place carpet designs on the right footing for the future. There can be little doubt that we owe most of these faults to the false taste of the designers in these royal establishments, who have vitiated the judgment of the public. Carpets issued from them are found which combine a mixture of ornament with natural or imitative flowers, designed with the greatest skill, coloured with the tints of nature, and gracefully and tastefully disposed. The ornament, however, is purely architectural, and in shaded relief, without any sense of flatness; and consists largely of the broken curves, the coarse scrolls, and the shell forms of the Louis Quinze period. The contrasts of colour, both as to tints and light and dark, are, however, sometimes of the most violent kind, distressing the eye, and distracting the attention from any works which might be in juxtaposition with them. It may be said that these carpets, designed for the gorgeous magnificence of palaces, can hardly come under sober rules; that they are essentially intended for display. Even allowing this to be the case, such specimens may well serve as warnings of the danger of adopting the like style for more general uses; and even in a palace, the chaste simplicity of its statues, and the subdued hues of the works of high art which should adorn it, could stand little chance of vying with the richness and lustre of fabrics so over-decorated; and the princely inhabitant would certainly share the attention of the spectator with the gaudy carpet which covered the floor.

The manufactured goods of this class too often consist of such a confused mixture of styles, and exhibit such a total want of consistency, that it is at once evident that the designers, both at home and abroad, are amenable to none of those *principles* which have been explained as governing the decoration of carpets; the flowers are often far beyond the natural size, the colours are bright and gaudy, flatness is not attempted; in short, imitation and not ornamentation has been the rule which has guided them. A work of much excellence is copied in the accompanying impression (Fig. 9). In the carpet itself the border is about half its width too narrow for the centre, but this is not seen in the woodcut; the colour of the centre consists of gradations of a neutral red, the forms of the border are red on a dull white ground. Though meritorious in other respects it will serve to illustrate the error of indiscriminately applying the ornamentation of one material to that of another. Thus the design, taken from the excellent work on the Alhambra by

FIG. 9.

the late Mr. Owen Jones, and there used as a wall decoration, where its "up and down" treatment was characteristic and proper, is no longer so when applied to a carpet, since this requires an "all-over" treatment, or an arrangement towards the centre, a consideration which does not seem to have entered into the mind of the designer. The justness and truth of the Eastern style in carpet decoration and in the application of colour to such fabrics, and the inherent tradition of fitness in both, is well known. Turkish carpets are generally designed with a *flat* border of flowers of the natural size, and with a centre of larger forms conventionalized, in some cases even to the extent of obscuring the forms; a fault to be avoided. The colours are negative shades of a medium or half-tint as regards light and dark, tending rather to dark, with scarcely any contrast, and therefore a little sombre in character. Three hues are principally prevalent and largely pervade the surface, namely, green, red, and blue; these are not pure but negative, so that the general effect is cool, yet rich and full in colour. The colours, instead of cutting upon each other, are mostly bordered with black, the blue has a slight tendency to purple, and a few orange spots enhance and enliven the effect. The distribution of colour in these fabrics is far simpler than in those from India, which latter have sometimes a tendency to foxiness, in consequence of a larger admission of warm neutrals, as brown and brown-purple; they also admit of a much greater variety of colours than the Turkish. The colour of the Indian carpets, however, is so evenly distributed, and each tint is so well balanced with its complementary and harmonizing hue, that the general effect is rich and agreeable; the hues all tend to a dark middle tint in scale, and white and yellow are sparingly introduced to define the geometrical arrangement of the forms, such arrangement being the sound basis of all Eastern ornament.

The carpets and mats of Persia and the Levant are coming into great favour at the present time, and most justly deserve the high estimation in which they are held. Both in design and colour they are often everything that could be wished. One thing is certainly to be learned from the works referred to, namely, that bright colours are not necessarily rich or beautiful, but that tone is a great source of richness, and has at the same time the further merit of keeping such goods in their true place in the scale of furniture. No nations exhibit greater richness of what may be called upholstery, or more gorgeous costumes, than those of India and Persia, and the wisdom displayed in the negative tone and subdued colour of their carpets is worthy of consideration, affording, as it does, a means of enhancing and supporting the richness and costliness of their other fabrics and their personal decorations.

Almost all that has been said of carpets is applicable to druggets and felted goods for the same uses, and the principles of their ornamentation, under certain modifications, may be applied to floor-cloths and painted cloth for furniture covers, as well as to printed, felted, and woven fabrics, in various materials, for table-covers.

Floor-cloths are not so much used in this country for dwelling rooms as in halls, staircases, lobbies, and other approaches, and richness and fulness of colour are, therefore, in general less needed. The laws which regulate mosaics and inlays for floors will, in some degree, rule these works also, except that wood inlays, especially when large, require a design capable of being framed in its construction, and due regard must also be paid to the shoulderings of mortices and tenons, a construction obviously unnecessary in floor-cloths. It is, therefore, requisite to guard carefully against mere imitations of such designs, and more especially to avoid all imitations of carpet patterns.

CURTAINS AND HANGINGS.

The ornamentation of textile hangings follows the same laws, and is amenable to the same general principles, as that of other wall decorations, flatness of treatment and subdued contrasts of colour being the only sure guides.

The richest, and at the same time the most sober effects in silk, are produced as we have already noticed merely by the processes of weaving, as of satin figures on a tabby ground, in a self-colour; and ornament properly suited for this treatment of the silk is generally in good taste, and shows the full splendour of the rich material. Next to this, graduated tints of a self-colour, as gold on straw colour, or even ornaments in one colour, on a ground formed of the natural golden tint of the silk, where the contrast is not too violent, have a good effect, and show to advantage beside those over-decorated works which are covered with natural flowers in many colours. In such treatments as these the lustre and gloss of the silk, and the richness of colour consequent on these qualities, are seen to the greatest advantage in the flat masses of such ornament, heightened as they are by the duller ground; while smaller parts and varied tints interfere with these inherent qualities of the material.

The *natural* treatment of flowers as the ornament of textile fabrics is nowhere seen to greater disadvantage than in the rich altar-cloths in gold brocade of French, Austrian, and Russian manufacture. The coloured and shaded flowers instantly vulgarise and give a commonness to this essentially rich material; while diapers of colour, or a different texture produced by weaving, or silver threads woven with the gold, as in some of the Russian fabrics, have a rich and true effect.

The consideration of chintzes comes under the head of hangings; and upon these fabrics it is quite necessary to make a few remarks, since their decoration seems at present to be of the most extravagant kind. Overlooking the fact that the lightness and thinness of the material will not carry a heavy treatment, and that, in addition to all the principles which have been shown to regulate designs for hangings, the use of imitative floral ornament is peculiarly unsuitable on account of the folds in which it hangs, the taste is to cover the surface almost entirely with large and coarse flowers—dahlias, hollyhocks, roses, hydrangeas—or others which give scope for strong and vivid colouring, and which are often magnified by the designer much beyond the scale of nature. These flowers are not only arranged in large groups, but often cover the whole surface, in the manner of a rich brocade. Nothing can be more erroneous, or more essentially vulgar, and this would at once be evident did not fashion blind us for a time, and a feeling for costly labour and difficult execution prevail over truth and good taste.

Moreover, it is scarcely possible in such distributions of colours, whether printed or woven, to arrange them according to just or scientific laws. For although this may be attainable when colour is in simple flat tints, and subordinated to geometrical groupings, we find that when the tints are broken up and graduated into shades, and distributed with regard to flowing and naturally-dispersed forms alone, the due quantities for harmony, the juxtaposition of complementary and harmonizing tints, and the true balance of parts, becomes difficult or impossible. The present mode of ornamenting these fabrics seems to have arisen from the false spirit of imitation—a desire to rival the richness of silk; but the fact is overlooked that the texture, naturally light, requires lightness and elegance of form and colour; and that, as a *summer* fabric, richness and fulness of hue, which tend rather to a sense of warmth, are out of place. The true principles for the decoration of chintzes, on the contrary, require fresh and cool light grounds, with flat ornamental forms, either "all over" or in "up and down" bands, or diapers of floral ornament, on a simple textural ground.

In conclusion we may say a few words on muslin curtains which properly belong to this section. These fabrics should, of course, have a perfectly flat treatment, whether purely ornamental forms or flowers are used for their decoration. The best effect for borders is obtained by a symmetrical arrangement of flowing lines, which may be large in pattern, from the lightness of the material; while a diaper treatment, or small sprigs arranged with large and regular spaces over the central field, complete the simple rules for their decoration. It would seem hardly possible to err much in designing for a fabric which admits of such small variation, the contrast of the thick work with the more filmy ground being the source of the ornamental form, and colour being rarely used; yet, perhaps, in the whole range of manufactured goods, there are few more glaring mistakes to be seen than are made in the decoration of these fabrics. In the Swiss muslins, the effort seems to be directed rather to curious skill in workmanship than to taste in design, and some of the most costly goods are in the worst conceivable taste—immense cornucopias, pouring out fruit and flowers, palm-trees, and even buildings and landscapes being used as ornament. Even when this only consists of flowers, they are used imitatively and perspectively, foldings of the leaves, and in some cases the actual relief of fruits, being attempted. Although the same faults occur in English manufactures, these, on the whole, have been greatly improved in taste.

Except that curtains allow of an "up and down" treatment, which table-cloths do not, most of the same rules apply to damask table-linen as to white muslin curtains. The ornament of damask linen, arising, as it does, merely from the gloss obtained by various distributions of the warp and woof in weaving, ought to be extremely simple in form; yet even in these goods we find buildings, landscapes, vases, baskets, fruits in relief, and flowers perspectively treated as the details of decoration, while we have seen a centre-piece of precious metal wrought in the table-cloth where the real one is meant to be placed. A border of flat ornament, consisting of flowing lines or a flat floral treatment, carefully studied as to the distribution of quantities; a diaper geometrically arranged over the inner field, composed either of floral or ornamental forms, with a judicious interspace (the diaper being rather dispersed than crowded), and a central form, give the best general distribution for the surface of table-linen. Proper attention should be paid, in designing the border, to the quantity allowed for turning down over the edge of the table; and care should be taken, when heraldry and heraldic devices are introduced, to have them strictly flat. Landscapes, solid and shaded forms, perspectives, and architectural relief ornament, should be carefully avoided. Although the principles which govern the decoration of these fabrics appear to be simple and self-evident, there are few manufactures where a greater amount of error prevails, the nearest approach to purity of style being floral treatments, imitatively rendered.

In concluding our remarks upon this section of design, we may again invite attention to the different relative importance, in an ornamental point of view, of the various articles which are comprised under the head of the furniture of an apartment. These are produced by various manufacturers, each endeavouring to give the greatest amount of decoration to his own works, without duly considering their relation to other fabrics. Thus the carpet manufacturer ornaments his articles so showily that they outvie the hangings—the wall-decorator, or paper-stainer, his goods, till they emulate the cabinet furniture—whilst the upholsterer overlays his share of the furniture with florid carving, with or-molu and inlays, or with rich broideries of silk or velvet, so as far to outshine the rare workmanship of the jeweller or the goldsmith, or the art of the bronzist, the sculptor, or the painter, with which they are mingled.

All this arises out of error; each article of furniture has a due share of importance—a relative value as decoration—beyond which it should never be forced; and the designer for each should have this truth strongly impressed upon him in all his labours. We may suppose it will readily be conceded that the carpet, bearing, as we have pointed out, the relation of the groundwork for objects, should have a quiet richness of surface and texture, intruding in the least possible degree on the eye or the observation; the wall decorations, the next in importance, being entirely of the nature of a background, should be subordinate to the cabinet work; which, in its turn, should hardly be forced into undue competition with the skilful works in glass, porcelain, metal, or the fine arts, for which it serves merely as a means of display or arrangement. Yet how often is this order entirely reversed, and the simplicity of fine art outshone by the gorgeousness of mere furniture! Where the educated taste of a decorative artist is not sought for, this too often arises from want of taste in the purchaser, who selects each object for itself, and not on full consideration of this principle of subordination; but were the designer really alive to the truth of the principle, such gaudy and false ornamentation would hardly be applied to inferior fabrics. Jewellers are careful that the setting may be a proper foil to the more valuable stone, but those who have the means of richly decorating their dwellings often make such a show of the setting that it overpowers the gem.

CHAPTER X.

ON DOMESTIC UTENSILS AND OBJECTS OF PERSONAL USE.

OUR third group brings us to the examination of design applied to domestic utensils and objects of more immediate personal use. Although there is not an exact line of demarcation between such works and those more properly ranging with domestic furniture, the division is sufficiently accurate, and is convenient as permitting classification under the separate heads of:—

1. Porcelain and pottery.
2. Table and ornamental glass.
3. Works in the precious metals, &c.
4. Bookbinding.

It will at once be evident, that whatever is comprehended in this section ought to display the greatest purity of form and the rarest excellence of ornament; such objects should be characterized by the utmost refinement and finish, since they are daily under our hands, and continually subject to minute personal inspection. Their utility, moreover, should have special attention, and convenience and usefulness should be carefully studied. Here the ornamentist will have full scope for the highest efforts of his ingenuity and taste; and when working on the most precious materials, he may add by his labour even to *their* value and richness.

Moreover, in those classes in which use is a first requisite, as is largely the case in china, pottery, and glass, the purest forms should be sought, allied to the greatest convenience and capaciousness; and the requisite means of lifting, holding, supporting,—of filling, emptying, and cleansing, should engage the attention of the designer, before the subject of their ornamentation is at all considered.

PORCELAIN AND POTTERS' WARE.

There is hardly any nation, however primitive its state, with whose works we have become acquainted, that has not numbered among its manufactures some kind of potters' ware; rudely made, perhaps barbarously decorated and imperfectly fired, but sufficient for the simple domestic purposes of people in an early stage of society and civilization.

As nations advanced in culture, their pottery improved also, both in elegance of form, in beauty of decoration, and in manufacturing excellence; so that their fictile fabrics alone will often mark the standard of national civilization, and indicate the progress of a people in the arts of life.

This has been the case not only with the Greeks and the Eastern nations, but with the modern Europeans also, both of Italy, Germany, France, and England. It is unimportant that in Europe the improvement of these manufactures has, until of late years, been dependent on the patronage and assistance of princes, since, at the period of the first impulse to excellence, this was largely the case with all works of costly production. It is sufficient to notice that the pottery faithfully reflects the taste of the time; that its improved manufacture and decoration has been coincident with general culture; and that the style and progress of art, its motive and object, are as vividly depicted on the pottery as in the pictures and statues of the age. Thus, when pagan subjects began to be treated among the artists of Italy, from the revival of learning and the spread of a knowledge of the literature of Greece and

Rome, this change was immediately stamped as indelibly on the pottery of Urbino as upon the pictures of Raphael and his galaxy of pupils. In the same way, when the luxurious court of Louis XV. became interested in the manufacture of porcelain, and encouraged it with royal munificence in the workshops of Sèvres, all the glare and glitter of that pleasure-loving court, its debased art and theatrical prettiness, were at once impressed upon the works of that manufactory.

In this view of the ceramic arts there is much that is hopeful in their present position, since not only is there a manifest progress in the last few years in the general manufacture of porcelain and pottery, both at home and abroad, but there is also a decided improvement in their decoration. We seem to have nearly passed through the stage of mere imitation; the antique has been carefully studied, not so much with a view to the mere reproduction of the elegant forms of its utensils and of their decoration (too much the custom during the latter end of the last and the commencement of the present century), as, from the examination of the vases and tazzas of antiquity, to obtain the geometrical basis of their construction, and the principles on which the Greeks applied ornament to their surface. Hence has resulted an improved elegance and refinement in modern porcelain; and the beautiful details of Moresque ornament, or the richness and elegance of the Renaissance, have been adapted to its decoration on the same just principles that guided the artists of Greece and Etruria in ornamenting with their own national and significant ornaments the beautiful works which time has spared for our admiration.

The works of this class may, for facility of consideration, be examined under two heads, generally broadly distinguishable, without, however, having special reference to peculiarities of manufacture or of material, whether as hard or soft paste, as earthenware and porcelain. They may fairly be divided into ornaments and works of utility. It has elsewhere been said that manufactures may be so over-decorated as to be degraded into mere *ornaments*; yet when works are produced simply with that object, they may not only be admired as addressed to the purpose of giving pleasure by their beauty, but by their production they often sensibly exercise a useful influence on the general taste of the manufacture. This is nowhere more evident than in the beautiful and valuable porcelain, the present product of the Sèvres factory. Here we find the taste of the first artists assisted by the science of able chemists, and, under a judicious direction, united to the most skilful workmanship and manufacture, and the result is that the fabrication of porcelain is carried to the highest degree of excellence. The *chefs-d'œuvre* of this factory, however, are works which must be classed as ornaments, such as vases, caskets, chalices, tazzas, &c. The forms adopted, heretofore so rococo, are pure, and those pure forms are rarely interfered with by the reliefs. The details of the decoration, the modelling of the reliefs and the painting,—whether these consist of figures, flowers, or simply of ornamental forms,—are, in many cases, of rare and felicitous excellence, and of high merit in all. The finished perfection of these choice works must have exercised a great influence on the other manufactures of the country, not only by forming a band of workmen educated to perceive excellence as well as to produce it, and capable of giving assistance in many other branches of manufacture, but also by their effect on the general cultivation of the public taste. Nor do such establishments benefit alone the country that supports them; they diffuse, as we have seen, taste abroad, even into other lands. Thus the improvement of our own general manufacture of china has already been adverted to, and yet it is but justice to say that it owes much to the labours of the national establishments both of Sèvres and Dresden; not only from the fact that their works have in some cases served as our examples, or guided our manufacturers by the principles of their decorative treatments, but from the stimulus to improvement which has resulted from the contemplation of such rare works, and of that perfection which arises from a manufacture occupying itself rather upon efforts of skill than upon general production, and able to employ itself upon them irrespective of expense and regardless of cost.

When we consider the choice paintings on porcelain and in enamel executed at Sèvres, not only from the old masters and others, but original works also, we shall be sensible of the great impression they must produce on the workmen, and the emulous efforts of manufacturing skill they must call forth. The figure paintings of Ducluzeau, Thurgot, Beranger, Laurent, and others, with the flower-pieces of Jacobber, Schildt, &c., must be allowed to have exerted this influence in a high degree. In our own country we have skilful enamellers, but those artists are not connected with the potteries, nor employed by the manufacturers; in fact, their art is too costly for such uses, unless where, as in France, a nation pays for that which is of great value for a nation's improvement.

In England our china painters are rarely artists, and but few of them seem to have artists' feelings, nor until of late years have they had opportunities of gaining the necessary instruction. The painters on china copy fruit, foliage, and flowers well, but when such labours are original they too often consist of but slight variations of some stock and stereotyped forms and colours, which the workman uses over and over again, without novelty either in grouping or drawing. In the power of painting the human figure they are mostly deficient, and few of them are able to execute subjects of which flesh forms a part. The modellers also have been sadly deficient in knowledge of the figure and of its anatomical details. In both these particulars, however, they are slowly improving, and the introduction of parian and other materials for the manufacture of statuettes, which now forms a large branch of business in the potteries, has been of service in showing them their defects and in urging them to amend them. The Schools of Design established in the potteries, in which some of the principal manufacturers take an earnest interest, have been productive of good results, and, energetically supported, they will no doubt be of essential value to the workman and to the manufacturer.

In the application of colour to porcelain and earthenware the surface should never be wholly, or, indeed, largely covered; the material has a purity that should be decorated, not obscured, and due consideration of this simple rule would condemn a vast amount of bad taste, such as completely metallizing the surface of china by gilding, changing china into imitative marble, or covering the field of many utensils with pictures, landscapes, or flowers. The Greeks decorated their pottery in bands, introduced to mark the change of curve, or to separate the various surfaces: the eastern pottery is in the same way decorated in bands, or, where the surface is more covered, it is merely with a diaper, which leaves the material sufficiently visible.

FIG. 10.

The adaptation of the ornament to the varying curves of their vessels is most skilfully managed by the Chinese and Japanese. An antique Chinese vase in enamel for cut flowers, which is here illustrated (Fig. 10), will serve to exemplify these remarks.

Landscapes and pictures are almost always out of place on pottery, and it certainly is objectionable to cover the centre of plates and dishes with pictures and views; not only because it hides the surface, which, it has been before said, it is desirable to retain, but because utility would be better served by the absence of any decoration in the part which receives the viands, to satisfy that sense of cleanliness only to be obtained by the white unchanged surface of the material.

There is still another subject to be referred to, which consists in the imitation of the ornament peculiar to one age and one purpose on the utensils of another age, which are intended for totally different uses; or applying the ornament of one material to the decoration of another, which last fault, in speaking of other manufactures, has already been often strongly animadverted upon. The revivals of Wedgwood were, in a degree, in this spirit; and although they produced a vast change for the better in the forms of our pottery, and placed a salutary curb on the extravagance of the style that then obtained, they were but the resurrection of a dead art; and the funeral urns of Etruria, being inconsistent with modern uses, have a cold formality quite inconsonant with the feelings of the time.

The abuse of the ornament of other materials by its application to unsuitable purposes is shown in many ways in this fabric; among others, in copying engravings and pictures on various utensils. In one case we have seen the most sacred symbols of religion were used as the decorations for the borders of plates, while the centres of them, and of the dishes of the same set, consisted of angels, copied from an illustrated prayer-book, flying in the midst of a blue heaven diapered with stars. Such incongruities, improper in any case, are sadly and strangely inapplicable to a dinner-service. It has been well said, that "symbolical ornament demands perfect accordance between the use of an object and its decoration;" but can anything be more inharmonious than such sacred symbols mixed up with a festive dinner? Such incongruities are ever arising from unthinking imitation.

GLASS.

Among the many beautiful materials which the earth has yielded to the industry of man, to add to his comforts and increase his enjoyments, glass holds a prominent place. If we regard its use in the fabrication of utensils to contain the fluid portions of our food, it is most especially valuable, since its surface has the power of resisting the action of almost all liquids, and, as a material, it unites strength with extreme lightness and great capacity. Its perfect transparency is another rare quality, whereby the purity and clearness of the liquid it may serve to contain is immediately manifest, enabling the satisfied eye to minister indirectly to the pleasures of taste. Moreover, whilst it is one of the most cleanly materials, from its extreme smoothness and hardness of surface, it is also most easily purified, and its pristine brilliancy is restored by the smallest possible effort of labour. Besides all these varied qualities, the materials of which it is composed are of the least costly kind, and the processes of its manufacture are extremely simple; so that it is fitted for general use, and within the means even of the poorest purchasers.

For the purposes and utensils above enumerated, the qualities ascribed to it, properly understood and duly considered, will lead to a discovery of the principles which should govern its design and decoration. Of these, the foremost are its brilliancy of surface and its transparency, both of which should ever be preserved with the greatest care in all right treatments of glass. And yet, strange to say, these qualities are not only often disregarded, but there is a strong tendency to contradict and destroy them: thus we see wine-glasses and decanters, water-bottles, caraffes, and drinking-vessels of many kinds, not only with the surface covered with ground ornament, but sometimes wholly and entirely changed and obscured by grinding, so as to render them perfectly opaque: or, we have colour most injuriously applied to destroy purity, and prevent a proper enjoyment of the glowing lustre of the liquid contents; whilst sometimes the material is wholly or partially opalized; in the one case making it into a spurious porcelain, in the other into a species of japanned hardware, without the toughness and tenacity of that manufacture. Another excellence of glass is its lightness, as compared with its power of containing;

the maintenance of this quality is opposed to the heavy and deep surface-cutting to which glass is now so frequently submitted, especially in water-jugs and decanters, and in the pieces of dessert-services. This cutting is intended to enhance the jewel-like and prismatic effect of glass, but it is opposed to its true qualities for such purposes, and should only be resorted to in handles, stems, or bases, where transparency is unimportant, where constructive thickness is necessary, and where the grasp in holding may be aided by the facets of the surface. Yet it has been the fashion to carry this practice of cutting to an extreme, tending to vulgarize, as far as possible, the simple and beautiful material: in some instances it is even applied to the bowls of wine-glasses.

The more simple mode of manufacturing glass is productive not only of the most beautiful shapes, but of its best qualities: and blown glass unites thinness, translucency, and pure surface, to forms which combine the greatest symmetry with varied curves; that is, the sphere, resulting from the circular motion of the workman's instrument, elongated by the breath and weight, into the ellipse and its combinations. These blown forms may be ornamented by narrow bands of engraved ornament, of which flatness and symmetrical distribution are requisite qualities: in wine-glasses and drinking vessels the ornament ought to be reserved for those parts of the bowl which do not interfere with a perfect sight of the contents. Any gilding or enamelling can only be admissible under the same rules. In all cases, elegance of form should be the first consideration, to which cutting, gilding, or engraving should be entirely subordinate. The relation of the stem to the bowl in wine-glasses is another point of some importance. The practice has of late obtained of making them of such extreme tenuity as to produce a sense of fragility and insecurity, which is quite as great an error in taste as the contrary fault of heaviness and thickness.

Like porcelain, a section of the manufacture of glass is devoted to the production of what can scarcely be called by any other name than *ornaments*. But while the production of porcelain ornaments has been fostered by princes, and, through the clever artists attached to royal manufactories, has arrived at great beauty and rare excellence, reflecting back an improved taste on the design and decoration of the general manufacture, glass has not been favoured with such advantages. Even in the case of Bohemian and Hungarian glass, notwithstanding the rare beauty of the materials of the manufacture, the objects we generally find can hardly be instanced for the merit of their design. The mode of manufacture, by casting in clumsy masses in wood or metal moulds, and reducing by cutting with the wheel, is contrary to the best qualities of glass, which consist of lightness and elegance. This alone causes many of the faults of the manufacture; since the true characteristics of glass are lost, and are replaced by qualities too apt to degenerate into the meretricious and the gaudy. Thus transparency is merged in rich colour, and this, again, overlaid with gilding: or the surface is flashed with opal, cut away by grinding to the coloured under-surface; sometimes giving the appearance of porcelain; sometimes even that of the inferior manufacture, papier-mâché; whilst, occasionally, the whole surface is frosted by grinding, and tinted in crude colours, the appearance of glass being entirely lost, and only its worst quality, that of brittleness, remaining: whilst the forms adopted are often as inelegant and rude as they are unsuited to the material to which they are applied. This is far less seen in smaller works in foreign glass, but it is, nevertheless, the natural result of a wrong application of constructive forms to the material, and of an improper over-decoration of the surface: whilst it would appear that the true adaptation of such glass for the above purposes has not yet been obtained. Its use in the manufacture of lamp pillars, knobs, and handles, lock furniture, and finger plates, seems likely to be attended with more tasteful results.

When glass is used for large objects, such as chandeliers and candelabra, where construction is required, its known brittleness is rather at variance with the constructive application of the material, and it seems in the principal branches and supports to require not only a hidden metallic structure, but even the appearance of it to the eye, to overcome a certain sense of insecurity.

In upright standing candelabra the work should arise out of some other material as a base, and it is exceedingly objectionable to plant a glass superstructure on the same material, supported on foliated or other forms of the nature of feet. In hanging chandeliers a construction entirely of glass equally quarrels with the sense of security; the chandeliers of the last century illustrate the error of such constructions,—their long bent branches appear weak and brittle, and the full beauty of the glass is not brought out by the lighting. The present mode, which treats glass rather as a string of jewels assisting to hang up the branches, is more consistent with its true use and best qualities; for while in masses it constructs ill and has not its full brilliancy, lustre and prismatic beauty are obtained by loose pendant forms cut with proper facets, so that every motion, however slight, contributes to the splendour of the work by the varied reflections of the lights. In such works coloured glass should be introduced sparingly, and it should always be translucent, opalized coloured glass hardly ever having a satisfactory effect.

WORKS IN THE PRECIOUS METALS.

The design and ornamentation of works wrought in the precious metals deserve especial attention in this Manual, since in this sub-division we should find the highest *art* applied to the richest and most costly materials. Moreover, in such manufactures more than in any other the labours of the artist and the ornamentist seem to concur, and are often so intermixed that it is difficult to designate their several provinces, or to determine where art and ornament diverge from one another. Here we have a field wherein we may study the right application of each, and understand the due limits within which each is available for the purposes of manufacture.

However much, in the highest range of his art, the ornamentist may be merged in the artist, there is a distinct difference in the principles of the two arts, a difference which becomes the more apparent as the ornamentist descends from labours of such high requirement to those more strictly within his own province. Art has its childhood in a careful imitation of nature, and grows into an abstract imitation or generalization of nature's highest beauties and rarest excellences—still, however, imitatively rendered—and nature, thus selected, becomes the vehicle for impressing men with the thoughts, the passions, and the feelings which fill the imaginative mind of the artist. The generalized imitation of nature is the language in which these imaginative abstractions are embodied and expressed, and this whether the artist be sculptor or painter: the landscape painter even proceeds on the same principles, and endeavours by a selected *imitation* to reproduce the aspects of nature in harmony with certain feelings which fill his mind, and which he wishes to impress upon the minds of others. In its lowest phases art relies more and more on imitation, seeking to give pleasure only by the reproduction of beautiful objects or beautiful combinations, until, in its lowest development, art, if it can be so called, rests contented with mere *imitation*.

In considering in a like manner the scope of the *ornamentist*, it will be evident that in his highest aims he is assimilated to the *artist*, so that it becomes extremely difficult, nay impossible, to separate them, or to draw any line of distinction between the one and the other. Thus the beautiful shield which embodies the description given by Homer of that of Achilles, designed by Flaxman, and that skilful specimen of embossed work, the shield by Antoine Vechte, copies of which will be found in the Museum at Kensington, are at one and the same time works of art and works of ornament. From this high range the occupation of the ornamentist descends by imperceptible degrees; not as in the case of the artist through the more and more close *imitation* of nature, but by selecting from her whatever is beautiful and graceful, irrespective of her individual embodiment of these qualities, and adapting them to give pleasure separately and apart even from any wish to recall the objects themselves from which he has sought or obtained his designs; his effort is to give the most characteristic embodiment of those natural objects (viewed in relation to some peculiar quality, form, or colour, or some particular adaptation required), rather than to imitate; indeed he departs more and more from *imitation* as he diverges from the path of the artist to occupy his own separate province as an ornamentist. These are truths to be continually borne in mind, as they constitute the only cure for that false style of ornament so largely pervading the manufactures of the day, and already so frequently alluded to under the name of *naturalism*; consisting of the mere *imitative* rendering of natural forms as ornament, and which is nowhere more largely exhibited than in works in the precious metals, and in the affiliated manufacture of plated and Sheffield wares.

While it is not possible, therefore, in works in the precious metals, entirely to separate the artist from the ornamentist, still for the purposes of description their separation is marked with sufficient distinctness. A great cause of the faults noticeable in works in the precious metals seems to be, that they have received their design rather from the artist than the ornamentist; thus we have figures having no constructive connexion with the work ornamented, but rather of the nature of statuettes perched wherever a ledge or shelf offers accommodation for them: these are generally as *imitatively* treated as the material used and the powers of the artist permit, and are applied to inkstands, candelabra, and works of the like kind requiring a purely *ornamental* consideration. Many centre-pieces, racing-cups, and testimonials are treated merely as groups would be by the sculptor, although the lowest style of his art has but too frequently been adopted, and imitations of textures, chain and plate mail, and such laborious littlenesses, made a point of, rather than that nobler view of art, which, discarding miniature and strictly imitative details, seeks by grandeur of form and largeness of manner to make us forget the scale of the work in the dignified style of its treatment. Now, if it is proper that these works should be consigned to the hands of the artist, he is bound to treat them according to the laws of his own art, not only by a noble style but also by making them, as groups, truly statuesque, and combining the parts so that they form an agreeable whole in all possible directions of view. Above all, the *thoughts* which, as works of *art,* they serve to embody, should be such as are worthy of being illustrated on metals of great value, which, enriched by true art, are enhanced in worth a hundredfold.

If we contemplate some of the inventions of the artists, and some of the thoughts which they have wrought out, we shall be indeed surprised that such puerilities could be dwelt upon long enough to execute them as works of art, and still more that manufacturers, so shrewd as they generally are, should be found to engage in their production, were it not sufficiently evident that there is a large and wealthy public whose taste does not rise above such *art,* proved by becoming its patrons and purchasers. What can justify the employment of the precious metals, and what ought to be the more precious labours of artists, upon huntsmen and ploughboys, to render them with all the coarseness of their garments and the texture of their hose?—or who, but the givers of a testimonial, relying on the known taste of its receiver, would require art to be degraded into the mere imitation of a hedge-row occurrence on a hunting-day when the sport was successful; knee-breeches and top-boots being items as important in the group as the hounds, horses, and the portraits of the individuals whose goodfellowship it commemorates? It is such art in the more precious metals, employed on such thoughts, that leads, in the imitative manufactures, to the many paltry inventions which are found to prevail therein. Rachel at a well in a rock under an imitative palm-tree draws—not water, but ink; Burns' shepherdess would find the same black fluid in the formless well by her side; a grotto of oyster-shells with children beside it contains, not a light, but an ink-vessel; the milk-pail on a maiden's head contains, not goat's milk, as the animal by her side would lead you to suppose, but a taper. Such works are akin to épergnes with the hippopotamus and his keeper; or Paul and Virginia under a palm-tree which upholds the glass for flowers on its top; or Apollo dancing, supporting at the same time a glass épergne twice his own size; and inventions of equal or greater *novelty* wrought out with great waste of skill and labour. Even when we find really artistic works in this style, of which happily there are many examples, it is more than doubtful whether the ornamentist would not have been more suitably employed upon them in obtaining an ornamental and architectural construction, ere art was called in to aid in their completion.

It must be owned that our own countrymen are greatly deficient in the treatment of the precious metals as the medium of art. The truth seems to be that here one artist designs the work, and perhaps makes the model, whilst another is employed to produce it in the metal. This is an evil we have already alluded to in the case of furniture. Thus we find works designed with great ability, and modelled with much knowledge, and evidently by artists of great professional excellence, yet these works are completed in the metal with every possible littleness of imitation, serving only to degrade and vulgarise the art it is employed upon; and this frequently is caused by the surface treatment and the mode of execution, wherein imitation has taken the place of art. Thus the true artist does not produce the texture of the fur of animals hair by hair, but gives its general expression by some conventional rendering, by the indications at the parts where the skin folds, or by tooling to emulate the lustre of its gloss. In the same way true art does not imitate the materials of our dress by the threads of its manufacture, but indicates them rather by the shape and contour of the foldings. Yet in the works under examination the surface is often subjected by the workman to a most laboured treatment, labour without knowledge, which dwells more upon hairs and threads, upon details and buttons, than on the form of a joint, or the bones of an extremity: the one is a labour that requires no exercise of thought, nothing but mere dexterity; the other requires a workman not only educated into a knowledge of the parts, but who can enter into the feeling and intentions of the designer. This dwelling with complacency on mere labour, and this evident satisfaction with its tedious facilities, can only arise from the habit of giving the models of the superior artist into less skilful hands, to be completed in metal.

Again, in the higher works in silver the true artist has the boldness to regard the material, rich and costly as it is, merely as the vehicle of the art he adds to it; and that lustre and brilliancy, which is one of the great excellencies of the rarer metals, he subdues by acids to prevent the glare from interfering with the forms of art. To the eye, silver, so treated, might be so much zinc, did not the informing mind and the beautiful art enshrined in it at once bespeak the valuable metal which alone is capable of rendering such a noble return for the artist's labours. The metal so used serves only to display the art; but our workers in the precious metals have not yet arrived at such a state of virtue; the value of the mere silver is too great in the eyes of the public to be given up, and the full glitter of its polish must be sought to satisfy their desire for cost and magnificence. From the same cause it is, no doubt, that figures, well designed and artistically modelled, are loaded with toolings and burnishings, are matted and frosted, and have every other expedient attempted, to show the silver rather than to exhibit the art.

Another defect of the works in the precious metals, as exhibited by our English manufactures, may be traced to the same cause—the separation of the work of the artist and the workman in silver; hence casting and chasing are the means of production here, whilst the foreign artist himself uses the hammer and the punch, and beats out with his own hand the creations of his fancy or the inventions of his skill. Casting and chasing in their proper application are means only of producing and perfecting a thing, after the design and model have been executed: even in the hands of the artist himself they are but completing and perfecting processes; the work, as far as invention goes, is already done before it is committed to the mould; and the chaser does but perfect what the caster has produced, with the more or less excellence, according to the art-knowledge which he possesses. But by the embossing process, called *repoussé*, the artist himself produces the work by punching the plate of silver on a soft matrix, and continually annealing it in the course of his labours. By this embossing process the mind of the artist is working with every stroke of the craftsman's hammer; and not only does his own hand work out every characteristic quality of the surface, whether of flesh or of drapery, and his knowledge supply every essential detail, but thoughts seem to arise out of the very method and means of working, and each stroke of the punch may prove a suggestion leading to new fancies, or be followed out into more happy details. Even from the accidents of annealing—constantly necessary during the work—the colouring of the metal in the furnace calls up new thoughts, like those which arise in the mind of the poet watching the glowing embers, and the artist at once embodies his new-found fancies. Chasing has none of these suggestions; as has before been said, it only perfects: whilst embossing is to it what etching in the hands of the painter is to engraving. The very means in the one are suggestive in every stage of the progress; while the other is only a more or less complete copy of a previously designed original. One thing that we neglect which our French neighbours do not, is the use of enamels; and the varied treatments of surface by oxidizing, parcel-gilding, burnishing, niello, &c.

If we can allow such works as testimonials, racing-cups, centre-pieces, and others of the like character, to be given up to the treatment of the artist, there is still a large number of other articles in the precious metals and their representatives, having a defined purpose as utensils, and strictly devoted to use, which must belong to the domain of the ornamental designer, and be subject to all the laws of his art. Of these, utility should be the first consideration. They should be composed on geometrical forms and have a symmetrical construction. Capacity and mobility, in most cases, will have to be regarded, in connexion with proper stability and solidity; and it should be remembered that, as domestic *utensils*, they are not to be placed under glass shades, and therefore will require constant cleansing and polishing, and that, not at the hands of the silversmith, but at those of the butler or his assistant. This alone ought greatly to regulate the treatment of surface, which should be such as will best display the beauties of the metal, and yet not render it liable to injury under such cleansing. In such works it is usual to make the handles and knobs points of ornamentation, and this not improperly; but it should not be forgotten that they are to be grasped for lifting, and should be convenient for that purpose. And neither in these, nor, indeed, in any other part of the ornamentation, should the relief be so bold, or project so far, as to be liable to accident or lead to entanglement in the use of the articles. Some of these remarks may seem almost uncalled for, but they are really not so: thus it is impossible to justify large and florid groups of dead game, of fish, of fishing utensils, or the like imitative treatments, when made to serve as the knobs of dish-covers, or the handles of tureens; however beautiful they may be in design, or however well they are chased, they are not convenient for use: neither can the hand be safely brought in contact with the metallic toes of a pheasant, the tentaculæ of a lobster, or the twigs of a fish-basket, any more than stags with their branched antlers can well be laid hold of to remove the cover of a venison dish. Faults of this class chiefly arise from the natural or imitative treatment, which has to answer for so large a growth of errors.

In jewellery, used for personal adornment, the fancy has full play, and the invention need be but slightly curbed by a consideration of use, such works being in their very intention ornaments. Where precious stones are employed, the first object being to display them to the greatest advantage, the designer should be careful that neither gold nor enamel interferes with them, and that there is sufficient motion in the parts to bring the light into play on their surface.

A remarkable contrast in some respects to our own goldsmiths' work is seen in the examples we possess of the native Indian metal work, wherein the least possible amount of metal is so treated by delicate hand-labour, by exquisite pierced work, enamellings, and inlays, combined with such a thorough consideration of the treatment of surface by bulb-work, &c., as to give the greatest amount of skilled workmanship with the smallest quantity of the material; and even in their commoner works (inlays and incrustations of silver on iron) there is such a due consideration in the first place of beauty of form, and such varied and beautiful ornamental arrangements of the details, that they well deserve the consideration of the ornamentist.

BOOKBINDING.

The concluding subject of this section has reference to bookbinding, and when speaking of the design applied to this branch of industry a few remarks appear necessary to counteract a direction largely seen in the general works of the time. This consists in overlooking the only true intent of the art—the appropriate protection of literary works—in order to make it a vehicle for such gaudy ornamentation and decorative display as shall serve to attract to their contents; the outside garb being a presumed measure of the inner excellence, a practice not more degrading to art than it really is to literature. Such attempts induce the use of crude and harsh colours, and lead to excess in gilding; to heavy and coarse imitations of carved work in leather, gutta-percha, and even less durable materials; to perspectives and pictures on covers; to improper and inconsistent applications of metal work, and numerous other objectionable practices, which, as they do not tend to utility, and are opposed to the true spirit of the binder's labours, must be avoided if the art is to attain to the simple excellence of the mediævalists or to the chaste richness of the binders of the sixteenth century. It is no doubt admissible, nay desirable, that the outside decoration of a book should have some reference in its ornament to the inside contents; but still the details chosen should be amenable to ornamental treatment, should not be mere conceits, and, as has been so often reiterated, should not be mere reproductions of the ornament proper for a totally different material. Thus a painter's palette, with its range of tints prepared for study, let into the cover, can hardly be regarded as the appropriate binding for a work on colour, apart from the impossibility of any symmetrical arrangement of the object itself, or of the tints upon it, for its newly adopted purpose. Neither is the perspective delineation of the apse of a cathedral a proper ornamentation for the cover of a "Church Service," any more than the host of treatments in the same direction, consisting of the fronts of cathedrals, oriel and rose windows, and stone tracery of many kinds, so often adopted for such purposes.

In all tooled work and block impressions, bookbinding requires flatness of treatment as one of its first principles; interiors of churches, perspectives of tunnels, and even figures, pictorially used, are quite out of place. Heraldry and heraldic devices should be displayed flat, and even strap-work, or mere combinations of lines, should not be arranged so as to give the appearance of projection, any more than coloured materials or mosaics should give the appearance of relief, although the fine old Grolier bindings and other works of the Renaissance period sometimes offend against this rule.

Another class of errors arise from mere imitation of details without full consideration of their intent and use. Thus, formerly, when the heavy Church Services were really bound in boards richly ornamented, hinges were a necessary appendage, as also were bosses, which by their projection beyond the surface served to protect any delicate carving, rich tooling, or rare metal work inlaid into the cover; and, at present, in books of constant use, of large size, which require great strength, and come under the same conditions, the use of these appendages is desirable and appropriate. But that which is proper for a copy of the Scriptures or a Church Service for the lectern, is hardly suitable for a book for the pocket; yet these miniature works are *ornamented* with hinges and bosses, sometimes really in metal, and sometimes only imitated as tooled work on the surface of the leather.

CHAPTER XI.

ON THE DECORATION OF GARMENT FABRICS.

PERHAPS there is no subject which comes under review in this Manual of more importance than the consideration of design as applied to garment fabrics, since the amount of skill and labour engaged in their production forms so large a part of the industry of the world. Moreover, the design applied to apparel must exercise a great influence over the general taste of the public, and persons who have been accustomed to consider gaudy, florid, and large ornament suitable for articles of clothing, will hardly be capable of judging correctly of what is true, beautiful, and appropriate, in the ornament of the domestic utensils and furniture of their dwellings. The great sources of error in designing for garment fabrics are over-ornamentation, and attracting undue attention to the ornament—which may arise from many causes; thus from the violence of contrast either of light and dark, or of colour, from overcharging the colour, or from the ornament being too large for the fabric. All these causes, however, are modified by the material. Thus muslins and barèges will bear more pronounced contrasts than the more solid or more absorbent textures of jacquonet muslins or de-laines. Silks and de-laines, again, will bear greater fulness of colour than the drier surface of cotton; while woven patterns in silk, formed by tabby and satin in a self colour, will bear much larger figures than are applicable to either woven patterns in varied colours, or the same pattern printed on cottons or silks. Thus, the pattern inserted (Fig. 11)—half the size of the original—is from a printed barège, and will give the largest scale of pattern which appears suitable for the open texture of this material; it would, however, even in the reduced size of the woodcut, be far too large for a Swiss cambric, although it might be even larger than the original size of the pattern on a self-coloured, figured silk. These observations will show the necessity there is for careful atten-

FIG. 11.

tion on the part of the designer to texture, lustre, &c., in preparing his design, and will illustrate the difficulty of adopting the ornament of one fabric for the decoration of another. The flowing lines, agreeable distribution, and flat treatment of the details will illustrate other points in these remarks. See also the pattern of a de-laine (Fig. 12), and of a muslin (Fig. 16). Though the relative scale of the pattern is a most important consideration, it is difficult, even after the above considerations, to arrive at any absolute rule on the subject, since the person and the stature of the wearer of a garment must have some weight in determining the suitable size of the pattern. Generally speaking, however, ornament for such fabrics should consist of small, rather than of large forms—should be treated flatly, and without light and shade—and inclined to subdued contrasts of colour, and of light and dark. A geometrical rather than a dispersed* arrangement of the forms, moreover, would be found the most agreeable to the eye, and the most consistent with sound principles; some of the best patterns being formed by diapering sprigs, leaves, flowers, or often even simple geometrical forms, regularly over the ground. That such patterns are essentially in good taste is shown by their constant reproduction for the more cultivated class of customers; whilst the sprawling trails, and coarse imitative treatments brought out from year to year as the novelties of the season, pass away and are forgotten, or are thrust cheaply on the market at a low cost, to catch persons whose taste is regulated by their pockets, rather than by their cultivated senses. The above principles are nowhere more fully and completely carried out than in the garment fabrics of India: these are almost wholly designed on the principles here presumed to be just ones; the ornament is always flat and without shadow; natural flowers are never used imitatively, or perspectively, but are conventionalized by being displayed flat and according to a symmetrical arrangement; and all other objects, even animals and birds, when used as ornament, are reduced to their simplest flat form. When colour is added, it is usually rendered by the simple local hue, often bordered with a darker shade of the colour to give it a clearer expression; but the shades of the flower are rarely introduced. If we look at the details of the Indian patterns we shall be surprised at their extreme simplicity, and be led to wonder at their rich and satisfactory effect; it will soon be evident, however, that their beauty results entirely from adherence to the principles above described. The parts themselves are often poor, ill-drawn,

* By dispersed, is meant the attempt to distribute the pattern over the ground, without any apparent arrangement.

and commonplace, yet from the knowledge of the designer, the due attention paid to the just ornamentation of the fabric, and the refined delicacy evident in the selection of *quantity*, and the choice of tints, both for the ground, where gold is not used as a ground, and for the ornamental forms, the fabrics, individually, and as a whole, will give many useful lessons to our designers and manufacturers. Moreover, in the adaptation of all these qualities of design to the fabrics for which they are intended there is an entire appreciation of the effects to be produced by the texture and foldings of the tissue when in use as an article of dress, insomuch that no draught of the design can be made in any way to show the full beauty of the manufactured article, since this is only called out by the motion and folding of the fabric itself.

In reverting to the general question of design for garment fabrics, it may be remarked that the making up of such goods for use should have due consideration in the general direction of the pattern. Thus while, "up and down" treatments in stripes and trails are proper, the horizontal direction of pronounced forms is not to be admitted, since, as they must cross the person, the pattern would quarrel with all the motions of the human figure, as well as with the form of the long folds in the skirts of the garment; for this reason, large and pronounced checks, however fashionable, are often in very bad taste, and interfere with the graceful arrangement of any material as drapery.

In designing for garment fabrics, it will generally be found that the simplest patterns are in the best taste. The efforts, however, both of designers and manufacturers, have been too often directed towards difficulty and complication, rather than to produce the greatest effect with the least possible means. Thus we find the number of blocks used in printing any pattern, or of colours in weaving, or the number of cards required to produce a certain design, dwelt upon, rather than the excellence of the design itself, and gaudiness and ugliness are estimated, if expensive and troublesome in production, rather than beautiful simplicity at small cost. As simplicity is one of the first constituents of beauty, it will often happen that simple patterns are far the most beautiful, and that the effect of one printing, or weaving in one colour, is in good taste, while every multiplied difficulty becomes further removed from it. It has before been said, that calling undue attention to the ornament is a great error in designing for garment fabrics: there needs, in the larger masses of the dress, a sense of what a painter calls *breadth* or repose, which is only attainable by great simplicity, by flat or diapered treatments of small forms, by uncontrasted light and dark, and delicate tints of colour: those complicated patterns of many parts are too apt to offend against the above requirements, and to cause the figure to stare upon its ground and attract attention to itself, to the destruction of the true decoration of such fabrics.

In the section on the precious metals it has been stated that imitation is not one of the principles of ornamental art generally, but rather one of the elementary bases of fine art, and it is now desirable to give another distinctive difference between the two which will serve still more to define their respective provinces. It is, that geometry, not necessary as a principle of art, is essentially required as the basis of ornament; thus the grouping and arrangement of art is picturesque and dissymmetrical, and consists rather of unequal quantities, except in some of the works of the early artists, which had an ornamental source. Ornament, on the contrary, has a geometrical distribution, and is subject to symmetry and correspondence of parts, and it may be truly said that it is from confounding these provinces, and a departure from this true foundation on the part of the ornamentist, that has caused so much bad ornament in various branches of our manufactures, and in none more than in the textile fabrics. Thus it is not possible to cover a large space with a repetition of small ornament, without *some* symmetrical arrangement developing itself, however studiously we may endeavour to avoid it, the necessary "repeats," for instance, leading to the development of the square. In such *dispersed* patterns, therefore, some amount of symmetry is produced by chance; thus the pattern (Fig. 12) has not been founded on any geometrical lines, yet a four or five fold repetition would develop a regular arrangement of parts, some determinate recurrence of the berries, for instance, subject to a symmetrical law of lines. In such a case, then, the geometrical law of recurrence is arrived at adventitiously, the necessity inducing it being un-

FIG. 12.

governed by the controlling will of the designer, who therefore has neglected all the beauty resulting from a proper choice of the regulating form. Moreover, if a repetition by means of blocks or cylinders wholly without a symmetrical arrangement is an impossibility, would this not lead us to infer that symmetry is a law of nature not lightly to be broken through or disregarded, and should it not induce us to search for those geometrical figures which give the best distributions of quantities, and the arrangements most pleasing to the eye? In fact we ought not to attempt to overcome this law, but to accept it, and so regulate it as to give effect to other qualities essential to beauty, such as proportion, quantity, grace, and harmony of colour.

Having shown then that symmetry, regulated by geometrical forms, should govern the distribution of ornament, a little investigation would lead to the causes why certain symmetrical arrangements please more than others ; thus the square of equal sides and equal angles (Fig. 13) is the simplest and least varied basis of distribution, the most obvious regular figure, and at the same time the most inelegant and commonplace; simply changing the direction of the lines, however, and placing the square lozengewise, as

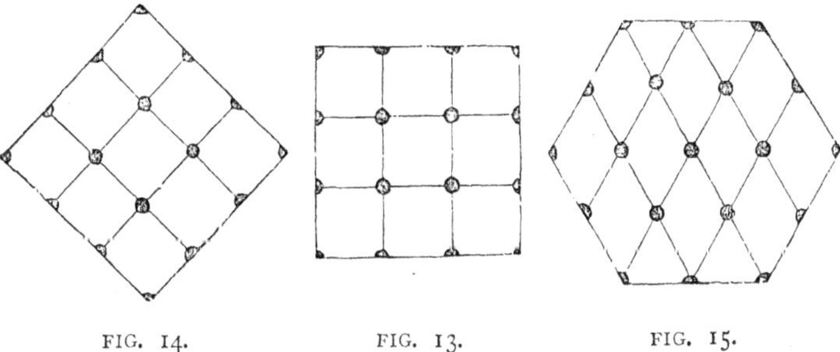

FIG. 14. FIG. 13. FIG. 15.

in Fig. 14, gives a decided improvement; variety is partially joined to perfect symmetry, and a more pleasing arrangement of the forms and quantities than in Fig. 13 is the result. Then again, if we not only change the direction of the governing lines, as in the last figure, but their angle also, as in Fig. 15, and adopt the equilateral triangle and the lozenge which is its plural, we have a further variety, in the interchange between the upright and perpendicular spaces of the quantities, and the result is a still more elegant distribution arising from the mere variation of arrangement of the same simple details. Having arrived at these facts as a starting-point, viz., that symmetry is a necessary condition of repetition, and that symmetrical beauty is largely influenced by the angle or combination of angles which govern it, we may pass from the right angle, and the angle of sixty degrees which forms the equilateral triangle, to study arrangements under various other geometrical combinations, founded on other polygons and on ordinate lines from the various intersections of the sides of polygonal figures; such as hexagons, octagons, &c., of an equal number of sides; or triangles, pentagons, &c., of an unequal number, developing many beautiful symmetries and proportional arrangements.

Thus the design inserted (Fig. 16), intended for a printed

FIG. 16.

muslin, is founded on combinations of the octagon and its ordinate lines. As combining geometrical forms with a thoroughly flat floral treatment it is very ingenious; the size of the pattern (one-half larger than the block) is very well considered for the texture of the fabric, and it will serve to illustrate the subsequent remarks on *quantity*, as the pattern covers well without being crowded, it is *broad* from the absence of harsh contrasts, whilst a sufficient amount of surface is left uncovered as required by this material. The colours, much wanted for the proper expression of the pattern, are delicately rendered in pink and green, and the design has a character of much elegance for a light fabric such as muslin.

Geometry then is the basis of symmetry, leading the way to those arrangements which best govern the general distribution of *form*. If this view of the value of geometrical arrangement is correct as to the distribution of *form*, it is still more so as to colour; some colours require definite arrangements in juxtaposition with one another for harmony, and are governed by their own laws of relative quantity, having reference to their power of mutual neutralization, as three yellow, five red, and eight blue; such arrangements being more easily obtained and regulated on a geometrical basis, than on those dispersed patterns which arise out of repetitions of the accidents of growth, or natural imitations.

The subject next in importance is *quantity*, by which, in the decoration of garment fabrics, the taste of the designer is so largely made known. The due appreciation of quantity regulates the amount of the surface of the ground to be covered by the ornament, the interspaces between diapered forms, and the size of the ornamental details, especially in relation to the geometrical bases which govern the grouping; thus in the Figures 13, 14, and 15, the spots which are regulated by the ordinate lines might be larger or smaller, or, instead of them, the lozenges might be filled wholly or partially with ornament, as in the design inserted (Fig. 16), the beauty and elegance of the design largely depending on the proper quantity admitted. Here the taste of the designer is exercised where rules help him no longer, but where he is guided by the considerations before mentioned as to textures of stuffs and qualities of surface, very important considerations which will be further spoken of. A study of Indian tissues will show how well *quantity* as a source of excellence is understood in the East, their quantities being generally extremely suitable to the colour and texture of the material sought to be ornamented.

To recur to the subject of textures and surface as important considerations regulating design. It is too much the custom with designers to imagine that the patterns applicable to one quality of surface may be used indiscriminately for another, and to think that something which is successful in one material, or by one process, must necessarily be a success in another; thus, no sooner does a pattern in silk or worsted obtain the notice of the public than it is immediately copied in printed cottons, without any regard to differences of material or modes of production, to the lustre and richness which belong to the former, and must be wanting in the latter. In adopting the patterns of the weaver, the progress by squares necessary to the weaving process is imitated in printing where it is neither suitable nor required; sometimes the whole texture and treatment is copied on the cylinder. As an observable instance, no sooner did alpacas make a strong impression on the public and become popular, than their low tones and broken tints were imitated largely in cotton prints, which almost changed their character from this circumstance, a low-toned surface or ground being adopted with slightly contrasting figures; they lost their own character to take up an unsuitable one. Cotton prints are capable of being easily cleansed, and the whiteness of the material is a great cause of beauty from its appealing to our sense of purity; this source of excellence is heightened rather than diminished by such a treatment of the ornament as contrasts with the general ground without covering it too much (see Fig. 16); when the ground, therefore, is entirely covered, as in these imitations, this appeal to the eye is lost, and, however suitable such patterns may be for the poorer classes, they detract from the true beauty of the fabric. The contrary is the case with woollens; the material does not admit either of the same easy purifying, nor has it the same native whiteness; the whole ground, therefore, may be coloured, or where its native hue is retained it must be more largely covered with the pattern. Thus Fig. 12 (page 138) is a pattern for a de-laine, and shows not only a proper flatness of treatment, but an agreeable quantity and a due amount of the surface covered by the ornament, and is therefore suitable for such goods.

The consideration of texture and surface is necessary in the application of design to other fabrics as well as cotton, and to other means besides printing; thus colour, which has such effect on printed woollen goods, and shows with such richness and fulness in the absorbent material of de-laines and flannels, where it may be used broken over nearly the whole surface, is apt to destroy more valuable qualities when applied in varied tints to the decoration of silk. Colour should be used more sparingly on this material either in woven or printed patterns, leaving large spaces of the ground untouched; so much of the true beauty of silk consisting, as before stated, in its lustrousness and the textural beauty of its surface. Of course this remark does not refer to self-coloured silks nor to figured brocades in a self-colour, where the greatest brilliancy of colour does not interfere with the textural beauty, but only to weaving or printing patterns, consisting of many colours, too largely spread over the surface! The fact is, that a variety of colours tends to vulgarize both cotton, woollen, and silk fabrics, and, although least objectionable in woollen goods, they want an attention to laws of harmony which either has not been given them, or is not easily attainable by those hues which chemistry has placed at the command of the manufacturer as comprising durability among their other qualities.

The proper treatment of texture has other considerations as respects the ornamentation of garment fabrics; graceful and elegant foldings are very important in all goods intended for personal wear, and many of the most beautiful qualities of materials are brought out by the interchange of light and reflection playing over their surface on the motion of the wearer. It is important, therefore, that no mode of decoration should be adopted, calculated to destroy this quality, even irrespective of the sacrifice of proper utility which takes place in all works so overcharged with decoration or stiff from embroidery as to impede ease of movement and freedom of action in the wearer: the full lustre of silk more especially is dependent upon the folding, and every fabric is more or less influenced by the same cause. When gold or silver threads are introduced in the weaving, stiffness must result from them, and the skill of the designer should be so exercised as to give the greatest effect from the least possible use of such materials.

The restrained use of means has often been before adverted to, nor is it unnecessary to recur to it in this section also ; under the old and simple methods of cotton printing, when the resources were few and the means limited, the style was in some respects better than at present obtains. Thus block-printing by hand required flat forms and flat tints diapered regularly over the surface, and some simple flower or leaf so used had a pleasing and just effect, of which Peel's well-known parsley-leaf may serve as an instance. It will at once be seen that these qualities are herein advocated as *principles*, to be filled up and enriched by more modern resources, yet as ascertained truths not to be departed from. In the place, however, of the former limited means, printing from metal cylinders has put at the command of the designer all those powers of more perfect imitation enjoyed by the engraver, and, instead of using them as they should be used, consistently with the requirements of manufacture and the principles of ornamental art, they are wasted on the *imitation* of flowers, foliage, and accidents of growth, quite out of ornamental character and opposed to just principles.

Generally, however, it may be stated that there is less dereliction from true ornamental art in woven than in printed goods, the powers of the weaving process being more limited than those of the printing process, so that varied tints and complicated forms fortunately present greater difficulties in production in the former than in the latter case.

SHAWLS.

In the section of garment fabrics, design as applied to shawls has been reserved for a separate head; not so much from the importance of the manufacture, although even for this reason it would call for careful consideration, in that it leads to the examination of the principles on which these fabrics were decorated in the countries from whence this article of dress has been derived.

The beauty, excellence, and costliness of the shawls imported into Europe from the East have united the Cashmere patterns so intimately with these fabrics in the public mind, that it has become almost a fixed idea connected with them, and it is consequently thought indispensable to the manufacture that eastern forms and eastern treatments should be applied to these goods. Thus for a long time such works were but mere imitations, and the invention of the artist was less taxed than the laborious skill of the copyist. It is due, however, to the French designers to say, that they have of late made earnest study of the works from Cashmere and Persia, not with an intent to continue mere imitators, but to obtain the principles on which the eastern artist designed.

There is nothing more difficult than to disabuse the world of a rooted error, and as the multitude, who rarely understand the true cause of excellence, have adopted the idea that the form called the *Indian pine* is the distinguishing characteristic of Cashmere patterns, this form is supposed to be necessary to the sale of shawls of this fabric, and it is therefore the prominent or leading feature in all the European imitations and repetitions of these goods. But there are principles of excellence in the designs from India and the East which are the real causes of this beauty, apart from any leading form, and, unless these principles are understood and practised, the forms alone will help but little towards the rich effects so constantly found in those works.

The Indian pine, moreover, is not present in all Cashmere shawls ; in some it is either greatly suppressed or entirely absent. Whatever may have been the cause of its introduction there, whether as a sacred or national symbol, or whether used only for the supposed beauty of its curves, its constant repetition in works intended for European wearers is, to say the least of it, a cause of great monotony, and implies a want of invention on the part of the designer, whose skill should supply some novel application of ornament to such fabrics to wean the public from this stock idea on the subject. But in doing this care should be taken to keep in mind those *principles* which are the true cause of the beauty of the Indian fabrics, comprising their treatment of form, treatment of colour, beauty of line, and due consideration of the material. The treatment of form is one of the essential excellences of the Cashmere designs. The objects used in ornamental decoration are always, for woven fabrics, treated quite flatly, as is the case, indeed, in all the Eastern and Indian works, whether these consist of ornamental forms having no apparent relation to natural objects, of flowers, foliage, or even of birds and animals. There is hardly any instance in which this rule has been overlooked. Moreover, excepting in the ground, large masses are rarely introduced, but large leading forms (as the Indian pine, before spoken of) are filled in with a minute diaper of smaller forms, mostly floral, and the beauty is enhanced by the graceful curves and elegant flow of these leading lines. The colours also are subject to a general rule; they consist of simple flat tints without shading, each flower, or petal, where flowers are used, each leaf in foliage, being rendered by one tint. In the best Cashmere shawls these inner diapering forms are very minute, and thus a broken texture of colour is given to the surface ornamented. The tints, where in large masses, as in some of the embroidered ornament, have rather a tendency to secondaries; thus purple, green, and gold prevail, and the red is inclined towards the colour of the pigment called Indian red, or in some cases to pink, which is a diluted crimson (a red with blue in it): thus the general hue has rather the direction of coolness; this is particularly seen in the carpets also, both Indian and Persian, as has been before remarked. In the Cashmere woven shawls, if pure tints are used, which may be the case, these tints become broken by the mixture of colour produced by the threads of other tints coming to the surface in them in the process of weaving, thus neutralizing their force and producing the same negative tendency; invariably we find that flat forms without perspective or imitative rendering, flat tints without shading, and single hues of the same colour, are the principles of the designer. The due consideration as well of the material as of the use to which the fabric is to be applied is evident both from the nature of the ornament, which never draws peculiar attention to itself, and from the texture, since, notwithstanding the use even of metallic threads in the ornamental design, the Indian fabrics seem never to lose the property of flowing in beautiful folds, and adapting themselves to every motion of the wearer, an excellence not so constantly present in the European manufactures. Now the French designers, to whom it seems clear that manufacturers are almost wholly indebted for their designs, although they have made much study of principles, seem either to have overlooked some, or to have willingly ignored them, either in deference to the ruling idea entertained by the public, or in order to obtain novelty; but novelty should never be sought at a sacrifice of truth. Let the designer throw away, if he pleases, the Indian forms—the Indian pine form, perhaps, the sooner the better, since it never had any symbolical significance with us, and it has long ceased to have beauty of line, tormented as it is into every possible variation from the normal form—and avoiding mere imitations seek after a treatment in harmony with European taste and feelings.

Thus, for instance, geometrical leading forms are sometimes used in the Cashmere shawls, and such treatments might be most successful in the hands of European artists, considering the numerous and varied combinations of flat forms open to their choice. The Byzantine tracery, guilloches, or even the graceful forms of the Renaissance, if perfect flatness were preserved, might be diapered with colour in the Indian manner; but the tide seems to have set in quite the contrary direction,—the leading forms of the Eastern patterns are kept, the just principles are disregarded: the Indian pine, exaggerated often to extreme caricature is applied not merely to shawls but to other goods; the diaper, moreover, instead of being flat, is composed of flowers often the size of nature, imitatively and perspectively drawn, and sometimes most elaborately shaded. Thus simplicity is lost—the principle of flatness is totally disregarded—the colour not being in flat tints, and the broken *texture* of surface entirely done away with; the result has a certain showy beauty, but it is meretricious and unsound; it may be the novelty of a season, but it is built on a false foundation and will never last.

There is a circumstance connected with floral ornament which hardly seems to have had proper consideration; it deserves, however, some attention. Many of the flowers used by us as ornament are not in a state of nature, but have already been subjected to another art, the art of the horticulturist, submitted by him to a process of cultivation which unnaturally stimulates the growth of the parts, and by means of which, the stamens being converted into petals, the flower becomes doubled and rendered artificial—more beautiful, perhaps, as a flower, but less tractable as ornament, and far less simple, far less fitted for that flat display which is required by some fabrics. By these means the five-petalled rose, the five-petalled pink, &c., become a bunch of petals; and if we would see how entirely some flowers are thus rendered artificial, the dahlia may be instanced as an example: in its simple state it has a single border of petals with a central disk,—by cultivation it is a cluster of petals, so regularly disposed as hardly to be distinguished from a rosette of ribbons made up by the milliner. Flowers in this state are already conventionalized by another art ere the designer takes them in hand, and the result is analogous to the case of the artist who copies the actions and passions of the stage, instead of seeking them in their simple reality in common life. Moreover, flowers in a natural state have simple and clear characteristics which they often lose in cultivation, and it is the difficulty of duly expressing them, as artificially changed by cultivation, that seems in some degree to have led to the false manner of treating them in the ornamentation of woven or printed fabrics.

To return to the consideration of the fabrics themselves. The *relaxation* of just principles is seen even in those which purport to be simply imitations of Cashmere designs; it is shown in the introduction of small landscapes on the spaces of the ground between the large leading forms; in representing in the pattern borders of ornament quilled or gathered in the manner of a fringe; and in rendering the spaces filled up with small diaperings imitative of foliage, palm-trees, &c., instead of covering it merely with flat, graceful, and flowing ornamental forms. In lieu of endeavouring to suppress novelty, it is most desirable to encourage it as far as possible, since true novelty is not an extreme characteristic of the present time, but it must be sought by other means than those reprobated; the designer must not suppose that by exaggerating a secondary characteristic of style into undue importance, and adding new materials entirely out of harmony with it, anything really beautiful and new will be likely to result.

LACE.

In examining the next head of this section of garment fabrics, which includes lace design, we must remember that lace is assimilated to certain other classes of fabrics by its uses as well as by its peculiar qualities; thus, to worked muslins, for instance, by its general lightness, and as being usually without colour either in itself or in its ornamentation; and to ribbons, as being an ornamenting fabric to other parts of dress. It is one of the peculiarities of lace that it is necessarily ornamented, since, without some pattern upon its surface, it would hardly retain its name. Its characteristics of lightness and filminess of texture should never be forgotten in its ornamentation, which should be essentially light, elegant, and flowing; all straight lines should be avoided, not only from the necessities of the manufacture, but because graceful forms are required to pervade its ornamentation. At the same time this textural lightness may lead into the opposite error, and the ornament be so flimsy as entirely to lose proper point and expression; and thus, where lace is used as a trimming, the line which it is intended to enforce or enrich be inefficiently marked from this very meagreness. The old point lace, worked with the needle, was often too heavy in character, from too equal a distribution of the masses of its ornament; it wanted less crowded spots to give value by contrast to the general surface; whereas the modern lace, from the object of the manufacturer being to cover large spaces with little work, too frequently errs in the opposite direction, and wants parts of more full enrichment to give point and character to the remainder. The border or edge, which in reality constitutes the true lace, should have the most solid and marked ornamentation, out of which should grow graceful curved forms, less marked and pronounced, gradually passing, in wide lace or in veils, &c., into diapers of sprigs or small ornamental forms over the remaining space. While the natural lines of the growth of plants may be adopted as the ornament of lace—for which they are very suitable from their elegance and variety—subjected to a symmetrical arrangement, however, in the succession of pattern; almost all imitations of flowers are to be avoided: floral forms being the rule; imitations of flowers quite the exception. The petals and leaves should rarely be filled in solid, but should be treated with stitches of varied forms of the nature of a diaper of texture, so as to give lightness, variety, and richness at the same time.

The great excellence of French and Belgian lace seems to consist rather in the more true appreciation of beauty of line and delicacy of form, than in any very marked superiority of design over the English. There is, moreover, a more just appreciation of *quantity* in the ornamental arrangements of Brussels and Valenciennes lace than in our own; the patterns of Honiton lace are generally too heavy, the forms rather too large and overcrowded, and the whole effect a little too solid and equal, although this partly arises from the mode of manufacture.

The English lace, especially the hand-worked lace, seems rather to call attention to the labour bestowed on it as a part of the excellence; the foreign lace, even when greater labour has been employed, strikes us as rather elegant and beautiful than as laborious and costly, from the more easy and playful forms of its decoration. These qualities entirely accord with the nature of the fabric, and charm us more when, on examination, we become sensible of the curious elaboration which often accompanies them. On the whole there are fewer errors in the designs for lace than prevail in most other manufactures, partly arising from its circumscribed nature.

RIBBONS.

Our concluding subject is design applied to ribbons, and here again it is necessary to have especial regard to their use, and the purpose which they are intended to fulfil; for although many of the principles which have been laid down as regulating the decoration of garment fabrics are equally applicable to them, these principles are modified by the place which ribbons hold, partaking, as they do, largely of the nature of *ornaments added* to the other portions of the dress.

It may be said that, when the dress itself has much pattern, ribbons, which serve as bands marking the leading lines, or as borders, should be plain in colour and without much enrichment; their office is contrast, and either simple colours or stripes in that case are most desirable; but when the garments themselves are plain and unfigured, or figured without strong oppositions of light and dark or colour, then the ribbon may become a true contrast by its ornamentation, and may require marked forms and colours to give that expression which is so requisite. When regulated by good taste, ribbons, besides giving effect to form by their contrasts, serve another important purpose, by being the means of introducing brilliant portions of pure colour, complementary to the general masses of the dress ; thereby, when the pervading tone of the dress is negative, giving that brilliancy and heightening which, when judicious, is a great means of enhancing its effect, and giving richness without gaudiness. This use of ribbons points out their proper ornamentation, which should be in simple forms, permitting the introduction of pure tints : these forms require a geometrical arrangement to give them adequate force and expression, and for this purpose the patterns of many Indian tissues offer most valuable suggestions to the ornamentist ; even the introduction of gold and silver may be taken advantage of as a very suitable enrichment for these ornamenting fabrics. It is to be regretted that the great prevalence of natural floral treatments in the decoration of garment fabrics has caused the adoption of the same style in ribbons, where it is more peculiarly out of place, and that the rarest efforts of the designer and the greatest manufacturing achievements have been misapplied to overcome the difficulties induced by this treatment.

There is an evident tendency to gaudiness and over-decoration in the greater number of these articles, and it largely arises from the above cause. The increased width these goods are now manufactured, and the wrong direction of the decoration applied to them, have greatly altered their character, and we find landscapes, figures, portraits, and all kinds of natural imitations employed for their ornament.

SECTION III.

THE TEACHING OF ORNAMENT AND THE EDUCATION OF THE DESIGNER.

CHAPTER XII.

ON ART EDUCATION IN THIS COUNTRY AND ABROAD.

BEFORE entering upon the present state of art education, it may be as well to revert shortly to the past relations between fine art and the arts as applied to industry. In the Middle Ages and at the period of the Renaissance these relations were exceedingly intimate; the distinction between artist and designer had hardly arisen. The great German, Flemish, and Italian artists were not only the painters of altar-pieces, neither were they employed alone in decorating the walls of churches with the history of saint and martyr, but they designed the furniture of palace and church, the rich services for the banquet, the reliquaries, monstrances, chalices, the splendid candlesticks of the altar-table, even the hangings of the rooms and the robes of the priests. The architects were often at the same time both painters and sculptors; and they did not disdain to design, and often partially to execute, the interior decorations of the buildings they erected. Some of the most celebrated sculptors were equally celebrated as workers in metal, as delicate modellers, or as skilful chasers; and their handiworks in bronze, in gold, and silver are still treasured for us in museums and collections. But gradually the range of the artist became more limited; those who practised as painters or as sculptors ceased to follow the cognate arts: the artist ceased to be the art-workman. The manufacturer arose, and then, in most countries, the relations of art to industry were relegated to a separate, and, as it soon came to be considered, an inferior class of artists. Yet it must be noted that all great improvements in taste may still be traced to the follower of fine art stooping once more to ally himself with the manufacturer, rather than to those who had started as designers for manufactures advancing to greater taste and skill in their branch of the profession. Thus, in England, where, more than in any other country, the two branches of art had become most completely disunited, it was to the genius of a Flaxman that we owe a distinct development of the potter's art; while to Stothard, perhaps in a less degree, is due improved taste in our textile fabrics and greater propriety in the works of our silversmiths.

Although this change of relation between the artist and the manufacturer had begun to arise in France, as in other countries, the disseverance between the two was early checked there by the wise policy of Colbert in founding the Royal manufactories of Sèvres and the Gobelins. It has been well said that Governments are bad manufacturers: a great truth as regards economy; but there are other phases of the question, by which these Royal establishments come to have an important bearing on the manufactures of the country; and it can hardly be doubted that the acknowledged superiority which Paris maintained for some generations in articles of luxury and matters of taste, and the place it held, and still holds, as the source of fashion, has largely arisen from the taste of designers fostered and the skill and excellence of the art-workmen trained in these national workshops. These are points to which we have already alluded in our opening chapter, and to the results which spring from them, we have more than once referred.

Added to the causes which have already been stated why the artists of France have more readily allied themselves to industrial art than English artists have, is that arising from the locality of their great manufactures. In England the great seats of those manufactures to which art is applied are far from the metropolis, in which our greatest artists reside, and to which they press from all provincial towns. Staffordshire and Worcestershire—a day's journey from London—are the seats of our pottery and porcelain works; Sheffield and Birmingham, of our hardware and plated goods; and of far the largest portion of our current jewellery; Manchester, Coventry, Macclesfield, Paisley, &c., of our textile fabrics. There, no one following fine art will permanently reside; whatever advantages the manufacturer may offer to unite them to his interests, all press to the great art-centre. But Paris is not only the seat of art, but largely also the seat of art-manufactures. Besides the Gobelins, with its tapestries, its carpets, and its manufacture of furniture for the Imperial palaces, Sèvres is within half an hour's distance; while the furniture manufacturers of the Marais supply not only Paris but France and foreign countries; and the bronzist, the designers for goldsmith's work and jewellery, find their designs perfected in the immediate vicinity of their own ateliers. In England the intercourse between the studio and the manufactory is divided both by time and distance. In France the artist can see his own creations grow under the hand of the workman, can easily be consulted as to every change and difficulty, and finds the highest class of instructed workmen close at hand to aid in the realisation of his designs.

Other causes connecting those who cultivate the fine arts in France with those who more especially devote themselves to the decorative arts and as designers for manufacture, may be found in the rules of the École des Beaux Arts. In England, at least until within the last few years, those who desired to become artists sought the preliminary knowledge necessary, either in private schools, or by studying from the marbles in the British Museum, and then endeavoured to obtain admission to the Royal Academy. There the works of each candidate for admission are submitted to the council, and, if possessing sufficient merit, the youth is allowed a term of probation of three months. At the end of that time the works executed in the schools are submitted with those first presented to the council, and, if satisfactory, the candidate becomes a student for seven years, or otherwise he is remitted to his preliminary studies for a further period of six or twelve months.

Once in the Academy, his time is almost exclusively given to the study of the human figure from the antique and from nature, and to painting and sculpture as fine arts. Admitted to these schools, the pupils consider themselves to take rank as artists, and since none can study there but those who have gone through the above-named long probationary trial with success, the students cultivate exclusiveness, and look down upon the outsiders who are not partakers of their own advantages. A great change, however, has latterly taken place. The numerous advantages offered, and the excellent course of teaching provided in the Government art schools have led many who intend eventually to become artists to frequent them for elementary instruction. Therein they obtain a degree of acquaintance with the best ornament of all periods, some knowledge of styles, and great readiness in drawing forms of ornament and foliage before entering upon the study of the figure. Thus many young artists rising into eminence and many students of the Royal Academy, are now well acquainted with ornamental design, and are using their talents simultaneously in the decorative and in the fine arts. But the schools of the Beaux Arts at Paris have always been far less exclusive than those of our Royal Academy—the admission of all who are desirous of studying art is more free and unfettered than in the case of our own institutions. There the classes for the study of the figure can be attended, not only by those inscribed on the books, whether as students or aspirants for admission, but by any of those who are devoting themselves to the study of art. Another good regulation of the French schools is also worthy of adoption. There the figure from the antique is placed for a fortnight alternately with the living model, new places being arranged on every change. This results in a more rapid and less laborious mode of studying from the cast, while a more careful mode of working from the living model, and a more direct reference of the nude life to the antique is also obtained. At the same time, that irregular attendance is obviated which arises in our schools of the antique owing to the fact that the figure remains unchanged during a whole session, while the student, even when not regular in his attendance, is allowed to retain his place.

But the real purpose in view in drawing this comparison between the two academies of fine art is to show how greatly the Parisian system tends to a union between the student of fine art and the ornamentist. Through it students in the various schools of design in Paris—both Governmental (as that in the near vicinity of the École des Beaux Arts) as well as communal —can freely enter and study in the evenings side by side with those specially following the fine arts; Paris, a city of much smaller area than London, offering little obstacle to their so doing. Thus the class distinctions prevalent in our own schools are avoided, and the youths feel it no loss of caste to work indifferently as ornamentists or artists, accordingly as remunerative occupation offers. This is aided by the course of instruction laid down for the architectural students at the Beaux Arts, which is really a complete course, while the instruction of architects in the London Academy has been till within the last year or two little more than nominal. In Paris great stress is laid on the young architect's power as an ornamental draughtsman and designer. There are in the architectural course, four competitions in each year in designing the figure and ornament; thus architects brought up in the ateliers of the professors of the Beaux Arts are highly accomplished in a branch of the art in which they so seldom qualify themselves in England, and they learn to appreciate and take a deeper interest in all the arts cognate to architecture than has until lately been the case in England.

But besides the more intimate relations which have been fostered in France between the artist, the designer, and the manufacturer, and those to which we have just alluded, which arise out of the rules of their schools of fine art, it must be remembered that for a century before such institutions existed in England, schools, both Government and municipal, had been open in Paris for the gratuitous instruction of the artisan, the designer, and the decorator. We have from time to time inspected the art-education afforded by such schools, both in Paris and in other continental cities, and from this inspection—from the careful examination of the works exhibited in Paris in 1863 at the Exhibition of the Union Centrale des Beaux Arts appliqués à l'Industrie, and from the drawings and models exhibited in the various international exhibitions by Italy, Wurtemberg, Bavaria, Austria, and England—we shall endeavour to make a few remarks on the merits and defects of the varied teaching to be found in them.

In the French schools for art-workmen no special course seems to be laid down which the students are expected to follow. They commence with linear drawing, both with instruments and free hand, but in the latter case, the clear outline and precision exacted in the schools of art in England is not sought for, oftentimes a bolder manner—a kind of black-board practice—being the only elementary initiative. When the student proceeds to shading from flat examples or from casts the use of the stump in execution is far more prevalent than the point, and the same is observable when he arrives at the study of shading from the cast or from flowers and foliage, or ultimately practices shading the figure from the cast or from life. This tends to great freedom and ease of execution, if at some loss of correctness and truth; too often, also, the study from flowers and foliage is confined to copying the designer's rendering of Nature rather than any recurrence to Nature herself. By this the freedom and ease of the decorator is arrived at, though at the loss of novelty and of imitative truth. Our English course of teaching seeks freedom through knowledge attained by careful and precise imitation, the French system rather seeks facility and fluency without such foundation.

And this brings us to the examples used in the French schools, which are certainly not well selected, or such as we should so consider. The students are permitted to draw from modern lithographed "studies for ornament"—from coarse, picturesque costume heads and figures—rather than required to make careful studies from the antique—from flat copies first, and then from the round; the fine examples from the antique by Reverdin being less used than those by Julyan or others of like character. In these schools also there is far less drawing from actual plants and foliage than with us, and many of the flat examples set before the scholars, both of flowers and foliage, are such as have already undergone one stage of generalization at the hands of the decorative artist. They thus neglect exact, imitative studies of nature, which lead the student on to work in our schools with like care from nature itself, as a ground-work for his own future treatment of it. Again, although the construction of ornament and the production of new ornamental forms is taught in the Government, and partially in some of the communal schools, no instruction seems to be given in the historic styles of different periods, or in the principles which should guide the application of ornament in the decoration of separate fabrics and objects. The use in these schools of the ornament of to-day rather than of well-chosen examples has already been alluded to, and it arises largely out of the nature of the occupation of those who frequent them for study, men more or less skilled in the decorative arts, and constantly following them as their occupation. To them a knowledge of the prevailing fashion is all important, and any new publication by artists of repute, or any decorations in progress of execution from their designs, are eagerly sought as a direct source of present profit, and of more immediate value to the art-workman than those studies which, if valuable in the end by leading him to a fuller sense of the beautiful and the true, might do so at the expense of his attaining facility, readiness, and acquaintance with the fashion of to-day by which he lives. With us decoration is the exception rather than the rule; but in France the churches, palaces, private residences, and shops, abound with decoration, both painted and modelled, and the workmen who execute it acquire a facility and skill inducing them to spurn precise study. Such men often continue to frequent the schools, and their readiness has a charm for those who are their companions in study, leading them to consider facility the highest excellence, and disinclining them to that careful and thorough training pursued in our schools. Yet there is no doubt that the more precise instruction required by us would act as a corrective to the weak exuberance observable at times in French decorative art, without depriving it of the rare manipulative skill in which we are deficient, while an infusion of the French practice in our own course might be equally useful to ourselves, and correct the common tendency to coldness and apparent want of inspiration.

An examination of the works of art students in Germany shows us that the course does not essentially differ from that of England. The student seems to be taught practical geometry, perspective, and mechanical drawing, of which we find good examples, the course of orthographic projection being very full. In freehand drawing the same clear and somewhat precise treatment of outline seems sought after as with us, and the early training of the hand and eye to correctness is carefully attended to. The shading from the casts is, as in England, rather with the point than by the stump process. In our schools, in all the early stages the studies are alternated; first, outlining from flat examples, then from solids and objects; shading from flat examples next has place, then shading from models and casts of ornament; flowers and foliage are drawn from flat examples, then from nature; the figure in outline, or shaded first from flat examples, then from the round, and finally from the living model; so that through the whole course the student has, as soon as possible, the *thing itself* placed before him for study rather than a drawing from it given him to copy; just sufficient use being made of the flat example to give him power to proceed to the round. This interchange does not seem so fully carried out in the practice of any foreign schools. Nor do we trace in them the use of a well-selected set of examples. It would seem here, as in France, that the choice was somewhat capricious, and that at times the ornament of the day replaced for the purpose of study those finer examples which should be derived from the antique or from the best periods of the Renaissance.

We notice also that in many German schools examples of relief ornament are in use which appear to have been modelled expressly for study, and to that end have been made so sharp and precise, so cleanly cut from the ground, as to tend to great errors in their use. The student ought to be taught that relief ornament should not be like *appliqué* work, and that it is a great fault to lose that beautiful quality, seen in all good ornament, of occasionally melting the forms into the ground. This error arises among the modellers from working on a hard ground, as a slate or tile—a practice discontinued in our English schools at the instance of Sir R. Westmacott, who early perceived the stringency and hardness resulting from it. Perhaps the cold precision of much of the German ornament, its cast-iron respectability and mechanical look, so opposed to the happy facility of the French ornamentist, may in part arise from these faulty models. We did not find among their works many examples from foliage and flowers, and the life-studies were principally portrait heads, often clever and characteristic, if somewhat prosaic, and with too much attention to rendering into black and white the colour of the hair and dresses. As far as may be learnt by the works we have seen, the object of the schools appears to be more to form good draughtsmen and modellers, intelligent artizans skilled to handle the pencil and the modelling tool, and able thoroughly to comprehend working drawings, rather than to instruct designers for manufacture, or to instil the principles of decorative art. For this purpose the instruction they provide is very suitable, while it is worthy of notice how widely this teaching is spread, and what small towns, or as we should call them villages, have their drawing schools.

M 2

Bavaria exhibited at Paris in 1867 a collection of works executed at the École Royale des Arts et Métiers at Nuremberg. They were very similar to the other German works, but more advanced, of the class in fact of those in our own art-schools, and carried further in the direction of the figure; many fine drawings of the whole figure both from the antique and the life being among them, as well as some very bold drawings of half-length draped figures, florid in treatment, and picturesque as to chiaroscuro. The stump is used more than in our schools, but with a result less slovenly than in the French. The ornamental examples of modelling were from exclusively German works, and modelling seems practised by a larger proportion of students than with us, while, as in other foreign schools, colour seems little attended to. There was the same apparent want of selection in the examples.

The few drawings of students we have seen from the art-schools of Austria do not greatly differ from those from our own, except in being more hard, respectable, and precise, from the reasons already referred to. There were one or two heads from antique busts hardly of average merit, and some models of ornament in red wax on a hard ground, fully bearing out the remarks we have already made—that this leads to a clean and hard treatment without much feeling, and without any union of the ornament with its ground.

As it is, our inspection led us to think that the course adopted in England is better than that of Germany, and can gain little from it, but that advantages might arise if, after the care and precision inculcated by the more elementary part of our course are attained the students were directed to seek the greater facility afforded by parts of the French system of teaching. This would result from more attention being given to *time drawing*, a practice occasionally enforced in our schools, and which has then shown how fully the exact training of the student in the elementary part of our course has given readiness and power of rapid execution. In many of our provincial schools the member for the town, the municipal authorities, or the resident manufacturers, besides the rewards offered by Government, give prizes to stimulate the industry of the students: perhaps some of these could not be better applied than by instituting stated competitions in modelling, drawing, and designing, wherein the students in the school should be required to compete in a given time; rapidity of execution being one of the conditions to be combined with excellence in the work produced.

Although the composition of ornament is taught in Paris, both in the school in the Rue de l'École de Médecine and in some others, one section of the English course is peculiar to our own schools. We allude to the section of "Elementary design," preparing the student as it does for the practice of decorative design by the careful study of ancient ornament; by the analysis of foliage and flowers, with a view to the new ornamental forms to be derived from them; and by the study of the geometrical and other laws which govern the agreeable distribution of ornamental details, either as to form, colour, quantity, or symmetrical combinations. Two woodcuts are here given as examples of this mode of analysis. In the first (Fig. 17) is a sketch of a plant the Sonchus or sow-thistle) pictorially drawn as it grows; in the second (Fig. 18), the plant is displayed and flattened, whilst the form of the buds, the open blossoms, the seed vessels and the leaves, are examined as new motives for ornament. These drawings are mere indications of the mode of analysis, since many figures would be wanted to show all that could be obtained from this single plant; thus the setting of the leaf on the stem is remarkable, and in most plants the bracts and spathes should be studied, especially with regard to new forms of beauty in relief ornament; such study will open out original treatments not to be obtained by copying former ornamental renderings. After this stage of "Elementary design" comes the study of "filling given spaces" with the ornament derived from the above sources, then the "repeats," by which units of ornament are distributed over large surfaces, and, finally, the student is taught the proper application of ornament to the various materials in which the design is intended to be wrought or executed; these laws of *fitness* in

FIG. 17.

application are, to say the least, not followed by Continental decorative artists. The flat treatment of ornament on hangings, carpets, &c.; the conventional rather than the imitative rendering of flowers and foliage, the absence of shadows, and the true relation between the ornament and the ground on which it is

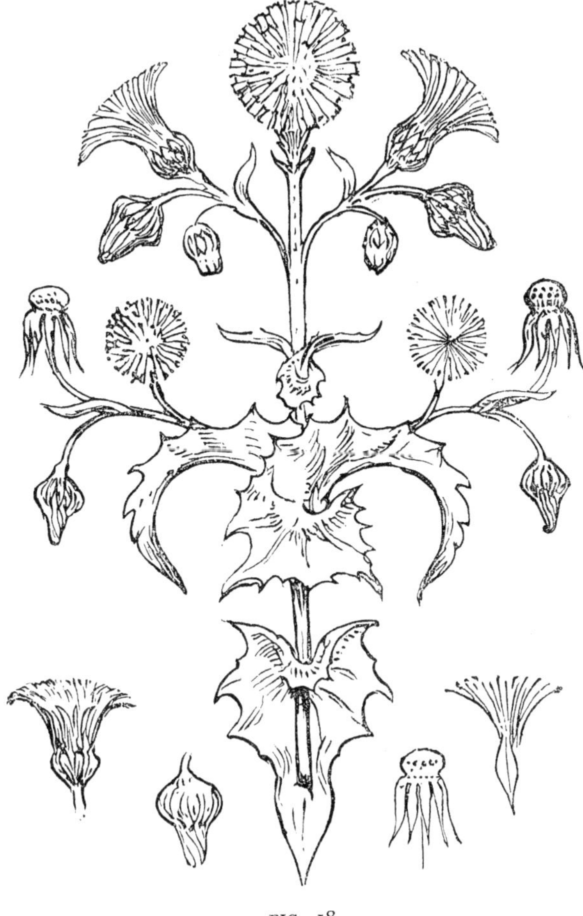

FIG. 18.

wrought—all so well understood by the Orientals and by the artists of the Middle Ages—are far too much ignored in the works of modern designers, and the true distinction between pictorial and ornamental art is quite overlooked. Thus, as we have seen, landscapes, animals, and figure-subjects are found not only on hangings and carpets, but on the backs and seats of couches and chairs, while the woven and painted flowers on the dresses of the ladies vie with the artificial ones that adorn their head-dresses, or with the natural flowers that compose their bouquets.

CHAPTER XIII.

ON THE SPECIAL EDUCATION OF THE DESIGNER.

HAVING thus glanced at the subject of art education at home and abroad, it only remains for us, in connection with our present subject, to consider briefly whether the means adopted in our own Government schools are those best adapted for education in design, or whether it would be desirable to extend their scope, so as to make them not only schools of design, but in some degree workshops, where the specialities of design may be fully explained, and the due application of ornamental art to manufacture may be thoroughly exemplified and carried into practice.

This question, however, is twofold, and has reference to two classes, whose functions and qualifications are not necessarily identical—the designer and the art-workman. That the designer should be acquainted with certain of the means of production and the peculiar processes of the manufacture for which he designs can be doubted by no one, since, without a knowledge of the *general* conditions of the manufacture his art is to be employed upon, his labours would be useless. But the question is one of amount, and the consideration to be arrived at is, shall this knowledge be given in the course of his art-education? or is it best acquired when, having obtained a thorough knowledge of ornament, he turns his attention to some *special application* of his powers?

That the art-workman should know *all* the processes of the

manufacture he is engaged upon is absolutely necessary; it is his starting-point; as his education in the technicalities or processes of ornamental art is the starting point of the designer. What the art-workman has to add to his manufacturing knowledge is, such an amount of art as will enable him thoroughly to appreciate and perfectly to carry out the work of the designer, without which, indeed, he is imperfectly educated in his trade; while, on the contrary, the designer (not necessarily a workman) has to obtain such an insight into the processes of the workman or the machine as will enable him to fit his design to the difficulties of production. Like the artist or the ornamentist, the two classes, whilst generally distinct, sometimes merge the one into the other, from which cause the question has been unnecessarily obscured. The truth is, that while, in *some cases*, it would be most desirable that the designer should understand the *minute* specialties of the manufacture, in others it is nearly unnecessary: while the art-workman's province is quite apart from the imaginative, and all that *he* requires is a full acquaintance with the *technical means* of art, such as drawing, modelling, chasing, painting, &c. In these he cannot be too fully educated; but since the large mass of those who are to be instructed are of this class, it is obvious that the principles and practice of *design* need not necessarily form a part of the education in *all* schools of ornamental art.

This view of the question does not interfere with those *special* cases so often alluded to in this manual, wherein, from the high requirements of the material, or of the object itself, the artist-designer is at the same time the artist-workman also, and produces and embodies his own conceptions by his own skilled handicraft.

The general truth seems to be that, when a designer has thoroughly mastered the technical language of art, and the general principles of design and its application, the amount of *special* knowledge sufficient for *his* purpose is speedily acquired in any branch of manufacture to which he may devote his attention; and in all cases more strict adaptation to uses, more originality, and greater aptness to mould the power of production to the best and most beautiful results, will arise rather from a full insight into the means at the manufacturer's command than from any technical education in those means.

This, however, is not the case with the art-workman; to give him proper instruction in *carving*, *chasing*, *embossing*, *painting*, &c., it should go on consecutively with his acquisition of the technical elements of art, and his perfection as a workman will be measured by his power of embodying his art-knowledge in his trade labours. The process, moreover, is a tedious one, requiring the hand to be educated as well as the eye and mind, to enable him successfully to combine art with handicraft; and it would seem, therefore, that such labours are essential parts of the education of true schools of *ornamental art.*

Yet the several requirements enumerated are partial and local, and not to be made a part of general so much as of local education. Thus, since London and its vicinity is the seat, more or less, of *all* manufactures, and of the highest efforts of those manufactures; for this reason, and as a central normal school, it would be advantageous to embody, in the course of the London head school, instruction in all such matters; but they could only be partially useful in the provinces; as die-sinking and chasing, for instance, in Birmingham, chasing and embossing at Sheffield, modelling and painting in the Potteries, &c.; and when it has been ascertained which are the proper localities for central provincial schools, their peculiar art-handicraft should be taught therein, and the instruction obtained in the surrounding districts should be of such a character as best to prepare for the higher instruction of the central provincial school. The truth is, that our schools have all been *accidentally* founded, rather than distributed on any general, comprehensive, and well-defined principle: and before proceeding further, it is very desirable to have some well-arranged distribution of the means of instruction for the whole kingdom, laid down in accordance with local wants and local seats of manufacture; and to control and regulate the whole, so that schools, when founded, should fall in with a pre-arranged and pre-determined system. These remarks are made with no intention to dogmatise on the subject, which should rather be viewed practically than theoretically, and the solution should be based on known results, rather than inferred from any supposititious points of view. The great public establishments of France, both of the Gobelins and Sèvres, would on this account demand especial attention and consideration, since the fabrics produced therein have attained a greater excellence, both of design and manufacture, than is seen elsewhere; and it would be desirable to gain full information as to the knowledge of art obtained by the workmen, as well as that of the processes of manufacture acquired by the designers in those celebrated manufactories. In the same view, the schools founded for the instruction of the bronzists of Paris, and in which they mostly obtain their art-education, should have a full share of attention, both on account of the reputation gained by these works for artistical completeness, as well as the great fancy and invention displayed in the Parisian bronzes. We have to learn whether the workmen have any, and what amount of, education in *design*, and whether their *inventive* powers have been stimulated, or whether only the most perfect technical acquirements have been obtained; we know pretty well that in the case of our own art manufactures the workmen have obtained but little even of the technical *language* of art, and that in invention they are entirely led by the designer.

The condition of the schools at Lyons also, and their routine of instruction, would furnish much valuable information on this subject, since, in the manufacture of silk, the relations between the art and the means of execution are most intimate and complicated. These investigations would show whether the education of the workman in art, and in many cases the exalting of him into the place of the designer, has resulted in a pure and just ornamentation of the fabric, or whether it has led to the skilful appliance of manufacturing means to the production of difficulties of execution in these fabrics, rather than to the simple and the beautiful in their ornamental decoration.

In conclusion, the author trusts that a proper spirit of inquiry into the sources of true excellence in ornamental art may be elicited from his brief labours, and that this may lead to the rejection of what is meretricious and false, and to a more simple, grave, and earnest style in modern ornament.

FINIS.

Published for the Committee of Council on Education.

SOUTH KENSINGTON MUSEUM SCIENCE AND ART HANDBOOKS.

THE INDUSTRIAL ARTS: Historical Sketches. With 242 Illustrations. Demy 8vo.

HANDBOOK TO THE SPECIAL LOAN COLLECTION OF SCIENTIFIC APPARATUS. Large crown 8vo.

1. *TEXTILE FABRICS.* By the Very Rev. DANIEL ROCK, D.D. With numerous Woodcuts. Large crown 8vo.

2. *IVORIES:* Ancient and Mediæval. By WILLIAM MASKELL. With numerous Woodcuts. Large crown 8vo.

3. *ANCIENT AND MODERN FURNITURE AND WOODWORK.* By JOHN HUNGERFORD POLLEN. With numerous Woodcuts. Large crown 8vo.

4. *MAIOLICA.* By C. DRURY E. FORTNUM, F.S.A. With numerous Woodcuts. Large crown 8vo.

5. *MUSICAL INSTRUMENTS.* By CARL ENGEL. With numerous Woodcuts. Large crown 8vo.

6. *PERSIAN ART.* By Major R. MURDOCK SMITH, R.E. With Map and Woodcuts. Large crown 8vo.

7. *MANUAL OF DESIGN,* compiled from the WRITINGS and ADDRESSES of RICHARD REDGRAVE, Surveyor of Her Majesty's Pictures, late Inspector-General for Art, Science and Art Department. By GILBERT R. REDGRAVE. Large crown 8vo.

www.ingramcontent.com/pod-product-compliance
Lightning Source LLC
LaVergne TN
LVHW011231110826
845150LV00006B/1605

* 9 7 8 1 4 2 5 5 1 4 7 9 2 *